Icons of
DESIGN!
The 20th Century

Icons of
DESIGN!
The 20th Century

With a foreword by Reyer Kras

Editorial Committee:
Volker Albus
Reyer Kras
Jonathan M. Woodham

With contributions from:
Volker Albus
Dorothy Bosomworth
Christopher Breward
Volker Fischer
Friedrich Friedl
Claudia Hellmann
Reyer Kras
Claude Lichtenstein
Jane C. Milosch
Hans-Ulrich von Mende
Hans-Heinrich Pardey
Ray Sapirstein
Josephine Shea
Courtenay Smith
Penny Sparke
Josef Strasser
Thomas D. Sullivan
Jonathan M. Woodham
John Zukowsky

Prestel
Munich · London · New York

CONTENTS

CONTENTS

CONTENTS

CONTENTS

At first glance, the icons of our industrial culture seem to have little in common with the icons of the Greek and Russian Orthodox churches, whose mystical and narrative images emanate a powerful message, especially to those familiar with their rich symbolic language. Why, then, is the word "icon" used to describe certain modern objects, and how is it that everyone accepts this usage of the word? In fact, most everyone can name examples of what they consider to be modern icons. Is it possible that some confusion exists in determining the significance of an icon or its function? Has the definition of the word changed so much that related and disparate meanings are acceptable? Or, could it be that some deeper connection exists between the two phenomena, something that everyone senses yet is unable to put it into words? Because *Icons of Design: The 20th Century* presents a selective list of the most significant industrial icons of the twentieth century, the first question to be addressed is whether one can legitimately refer to these objects as icons.

The origin of the term "icon" goes back to the Byzantine empire of the first centuries AD, when the emperor dispatched portraits of himself to the furthest corners of the empire, to ensure that he was not forgotten. The portraits not only depicted his likeness but also represented his power, despite his absence, and so symbolized the unity of the empire under his absolute and omnipresent rule. Analogous to this, even today a portrait of the head of state is often found in law courts as a sign that the judge administers justice not in his own name but on the authority of the state and in accordance with its laws. The early Christians of the Byzantine empire adapted this imperial portrait tradition to the sacred, investing their images with a mystical interpretation so as to convey the message of the new religion to the illiterate masses. Looked at in this way, these icons were more than textbooks for the faithful.

As with the portrait of the emperor, the religious icon supported a deeper symbolic interpretation. According to the Platonic tradition still current at that time, icons were the visual manifestation of ideas from an intangible, mystical world. The image and idea were thought to be identical to one another. Thus, icons were seen as a mirror of deep mystical truth. Anyone who worshipped the picture also worshipped the idea embodied in it. Within the religious experience, the icon functioned as an instrument of communication between a mystical idea and the observable reality. The icon within the Byzantine tradition was associated with power and authority and represented the indivisibility of church and state. This was reinforced by the fact that the emperor occupied a special position in the liturgy as a kind of intermediary between the congregation, the priest and the divinity. In this process, the transition was easily made from an imperial power to a higher one.

Despite their religious significance, icons soon took on another role: they began to function as a commodity, as a type of merchandise. They were often mass produced in studios adjacent to monasteries and sold as pious products. Just as production engineering and division of labour characterize modern manufacturing, so would one monk paint only the figures of St. Peter, while another reproduced only images of the Blessed Virgin or architectural settings. Some monasteries developed an expertise in depicting specific images that could not be found elsewhere. At times, local miracles served as a kind of advertisement, encouraging early Christian pilgrims to visit their monastery; the icons themselves functioned as an attractive travel brochure. Sales outlets were set up along the major routes travelled by the pilgrims, enticing them to make a detour. Aside from the icons, badges and plaques were produced and songs composed to extol the religious significance of a particular site. Many of these icons were bought in large quantities, some as souvenirs, others as tangible proof of the pilgrim's hard journey, and they were priced at all levels depending on the quality of the product. In contemporary terms, these endeavours, or "worldly" activities, could be defined as the making and marketing of a corporate identity, with religious pilgrims as the target audience. As with all trade, there were periods of prosperity and recession, of inspiration and plagiarism, of innovation and eclecticism. At that time, faith was so interwoven with everyday life and recruiting newcomers to the faith and active worship so closely related, that even the icon—with all its significance and functions—logically conformed to the rules of communication and commerce.

In retrospect, the most significant and notable aspects of this phenomenon—the Christian icon—were the following:

- There were two distinct layers of significance: the physical illustration and the image of an intangible idea. The two were thought to be identical.
- Icons represented and maintained the memory of an absent power and authority.
- There was an urge to achieve an ideal, accurate image—the *vera eikon* (true image). This could be termed the historical component, the effort either to recall or to preserve continuity.
- Icons formed part of a ritual, part of a liturgy. This meant that there was a clear and structured interaction between the believer and the icon.

- There was an emotional link between the supplier (the Church) and the user (the believer) in which both sides strove to preserve the continuity of the relationship.
- A well-organized pictorial language was used, making use of exclusive signs in the form of attributes recognizable only to the faithful.
- Some icons were unique pieces, while others were mass produced, with the necessary organization of production and division of labour.
- Besides being instruments of devotion, icons were also merchandise; it followed that there was a market.
- Icons included elements of recruitment and communication—based on a corporate identity—in the form of a transmittable, consistent religious identity.

This list raises further questions. Are the content and the interrelationship of these aspects unique only to the Christian icon? Is it possible that they are more widely applicable to the material world, for example to everyday items? When these aspects are carefully analyzed, with all due respect for the religious aims of the Christian icon, one is struck by the mechanisms in place for the icon to function successfully. There is ritualized interaction between the user and the object but also a specific cultural context within which the object functions. If it were possible to continue this analogy in greater detail, without having to fall back on dialectic constructions, it might explain why certain products in our industrial civilization are identified as icons. Evidently some products are perceived, consciously or otherwise, to hold qualities similar to that of an icon and therefore are accepted as such.

In any event, certain industrial products, like religious icons, make use of related mechanisms, so that the average person senses a connection between the two. It cannot simply be a matter of similarity in appearance or a matter of design, the differences are too great for that to be true. Nor can it be a matter of function as expressed in their method of operation and use. All icons are perceived visually, while everyday objects are touched and used for a particular task. Therefore, it is necessary to confine this discussion to more deeply-rooted mechanisms. For example, in the early Christian era there was a need for manufacturers of icons to establish marketing and sales strategies and to develop a corporate identity, to ensure the sale of their goods. From this point of view, there is only a slight difference between the planned production of Christian icons and industrial ones. Yet, however interesting these analogies may seem, they are still insufficient to link the industrial icon with the Christian icon. After all, items such as cakes, pencils,

cars, pizzas and alcohol are all industrially produced and marketed, but this does not liken them to Christian icons. In order to understand the "likeness" of the industrial icon to the Christian icon, it is necessary to delve deeper into the levels of meaning that are common to both.

We have already traced a whole system of intrinsic meanings attached to the Christian icon. Is anything similar attached to the industrial icon? If so, then by the same reasoning that applies to the icon, the manifestation that we see—the bottle, lighter, chair, car—is a kind of Platonic image, an illustration of some intangible idea that is identical to it. If we look at industrial icons from this perspective, it becomes easier to identify the intangible idea which it represents—its Platonic image. Things suddenly seem to fall into place, and it is possible for us to look at some modern examples.

The London Underground Map (see p. 50), seen as a piece of geography, is a completely inaccurate two-dimensional representation of a three-dimensional transport system, bearing no discernible relationship to any London street map. Yet it provides a perfect image of the London Underground as a transport system and of the city itself. In fact, the map is an abstract image composed of graphic symbols which are really only legible to those familiar with diagrams and blueprints. For anyone else the map is as much a mystery as was the icon to anyone who was unfamiliar with the symbolic language of such attributes as the sword, the key and the eagle.

Raymond Loewy's pencil sharpener (see p. 60) is an object that could be said to represent the American obsession with visual symbols of hygiene and health and Freudian masculinity and sexuality. It is also a metaphor for the power of Darwinian evolution, seen as inevitable, and for the constant urge for change in an industrial culture of mass production and consumption as seen in the United States in the 1930s.

The Swatch Watch (see p. 158) is a Platonic image of Swiss precision—an accurate measurement of time. As such, it has become an accessory available for everyone, regardless of his or her social status.

Each of the icons included in this book has a similar tale to tell. Each object that we see provides more than just an exterior view—a portrait—of itself; it is also an image of an idea that leads an intangible existence at a higher level of abstraction. To limit the scope of the book, it was decided to focus on objects found and used in everyday life. Of course, it would have also been possible to select only food products, such as McDonald's Big Mac or Kellogg's Corn Flakes; or to focus on fashions, such as the "New Look," the miniskirt or nylon stockings; or even trademarks, such as the logos used by Shell, Campbell's Soup and Apple Macintosh. In all these alternatives, the same mechanism is at work: the transmission of an abstract idea to an image.

Perhaps some innate mechanism is at work, influencing the way in which we perceive things around us. Yet, somehow this mechanism functions only in relation to a limited number of objects. Most everyday objects are no more than fleeting shadows, rapidly vanishing from memory, leaving no trace behind. But then suddenly an icon appears. This does not occur because of some premeditated plan or formula; rather, icons come into being through the catharsis of time, through the memorable events and collective human experience in which they played a prominent role. After a certain amount of time has passed, icons are equated with these shared memories and experiences. Only then, through the collective conscience, are they called icons. Christian icons underwent exactly this same process.

Industrial icons can also be compared to the secular portraits of the emperor which served to keep his memory alive. Even after the emperor's death his likeness remained a fixed image frozen in time. In a similar way, industrial icons are "time machines" that also keep memories alive. They are viewed as mirror images— true icons—symbolic of the nameless people and different cultures within which they were created.

In most cases, part of the myth vanishes as soon as details of the context within which the icons existed is unravelled. Apart from the icons themselves, the better we understand the intangible idea for which they stand, the more intriguing the objects are and the greater their prestige. This transcendence of the original observation is also present in the case of industrial icons. Their achievement is that they have not departed into history, like so many other products, but have achieved a lasting place in the collective memory. They have become unique historical markers, with a status far exceeding their original roles and significance. In their new role as icons, their original function is no longer important. To be elevated to icons, they need not have been the best or the most beautiful products of their particular period, because the quality they represent is no longer their own but that of an abstract idea. In some sense, they are every bit as removed from everyday life as the Christian icons.

This summary would seem to complete the search for analogies between Christian icons and industrial icons, but the question that immediately follows is whether these observations are capable of bringing anything new to the way in which we look at everyday objects.

In the twentieth century, the aesthetics and technology of everyday objects echo the great technical and industrial revolution of the eighteenth and nineteenth centuries, a mechanical revolution dominated by machines. The electronic revolution, which began in the first decades of the twentieth century, has reached a new peak in the last ten years. These recent developments have fundamentally changed the way in which our mechanical appliances operate. Certain functions which, heretofore, could only be achieved through the aid of a physical product are now unnecessary; they have dematerialized, vanished into the caverns of the chip, the hard disk or the digital network. The product as a tactile object is slowly disappearing, while function continues to exist and expand. It could be said that the function has taken over the physical presence of the product.

When considering the Platonic view of the imperial portrait in light of these contemporary technological developments, it is evident that the image is disappearing while the idea lives on. If the physical image no longer exists, how is the function to be recognized? How do we know it is still operable? In principle, these functions, like products, can not be equated with Platonic ideas, though they do share a likeness.

This shift in technology has also impacted how designers envision and shape electronically controlled products. Maybe a new approach, or solution, can be found through Plato. The Platonic world is made up of ideas that can only be accessed in the real world through a material representation. These images, and thus the ideas, can only be understood within a context of opinions, agreements and structured behaviour. For many new products, the image is no longer present because its physical carrier has disappeared. As a result, the context in which the object exists will have to take over the task of the Platonic image, since the function may no longer be apparent. Until now the task of the designer has been to create physical objects that harmoniously combine technology, ergonomics and aesthetics. If the need to design the product—the image—disappears, will that be the end of this profession? Or, will the designer be able to create an intangible context? In the future, this is destined to pose one of the greatest challenges to the designer.   *Reyer Kras*

The Underwood Typewriter No. 5
was so well constructed that its
basic design concept remained
unchanged for decades.

This typewriter is the most successful in history, setting the standards and style of typewriter design. Its impact lasted from late 1900, when it was first manufactured, until mid-century, when the introduction of organic, Italian-styled Olivetti machines (designed by Marcello Nizzoli) and the distinctive IBM Selectric of 1961 (designed by Eliot Noyes, see p. 137) set new standards. Over 2 million Underwood No. 5s were produced before the model was discontinued in the early 1930s, by which time almost all competing manufacturers had been producing similar-looking and -functioning machines for many years.

Used by journalists, office workers and others concerned with clerical work, the Underwood machine proved to be highly practical in many respects, even if most of its design features were not especially innovative in themselves. Unlike many early typewriters which printed from single type elements, the No. 5 adopted the type-bar format which proved amenable to faster typing speeds. Perhaps more importantly, the typist was able to see what was being typed thanks to the adoption of the "frontstroke" mechanism—"understroke" machines printed on the bottom of the platen (printing surface) and necessitated the raising of the carriage to view what had been typed. The QWERTY (or "Universal") keyboard had been introduced almost a quarter of a century earlier by Sholes & Glidden (although its machine, which appeared on the American market in 1874, used only capital letters). Despite the availability of other rival manufacturers' systems, this was the keyboard adopted by Underwood because of its widespread familiarity. The No. 5 typewriter boasted 84 characters, with 4 banks of keys and a single shift for capital letters, a configuration which was highly compatible with touch-typing and high speeds.

The practicalities of the Underwood machine eliminated many of the difficulties and frustrations associated with the use of earlier typewriters. This change is amusingly documented by the American novelist Mark Twain, while using a Sholes & Glidden model of 1874, manufactured by E. Remington & Sons of Ilion, New York. In that year he typed a letter in which he declared: "I am trying to get the hang of this new-fangled writing machine, but I am not making a shining success of it. However, this is the first attempt I ever have made, and yet I perceive that I shall soon easily acquire a fine facility in its use." However, a few months later, when approached by the Remington Company for an endorsement of their product, his enthusiasm had radically dimmed, for not only had he stopped using it, but he also claimed that it made him "want to swear." Ironically, the Underwood No. 5 typewriter might never have come into being had it not been for a dispute between Thomas Underwood and the Remington Company. In 1895, Underwood, a manufacturer of typewriter ribbon and carbon paper, approached Remington in order to renew his contract for supplying ribbons but was told that this would no longer be necessary as Remington intended to produce its own. Stung into action by such a rebuff, Underwood bought up the rights to a new machine and went into typewriter production himself with conspicuously successful results. In the early 1960s, the Underwood company was eventually bought by Olivetti.   J. M. W.

Frank X. Wagner

1837   Born on May 20 in Heimbach near Neuwied am Rhein, Germany

1855   Examination as journeyman mechanic

1860   Develops a sewing machine in Stuttgart that he industrially manufactures and distributes

1864   Emigrates to the United States; works primarily as a self-employed mechanic and constructs first typewriters based on the "Remington"

1890   Develops the "Wagner Gear" together with his son Hermann

1893   Patents the Wagner Gear and founds the Wagner Typewriter Company in New York

1895   Underwood, a manufacturer of typewriter ribbons, buys Wagner's patents and manufacturing rights; Wagner works on numerous improvements for Underwood

1907   Dies on March 8 in New York

Advertisements for Underwood typewriters, ca. 1900.

HILL HOUSE CHAIR

Charles Rennie Mackintosh

Charles Rennie Mackintosh

1868	Born on January 7 in Glasgow
1885–89	Studies at the Glasgow School of Art
1890	Sets up the "Glasgow Four" collective with designers J. Herbert MacNair, Frances Macdonald and Margaret Macdonald (whom he later marries)
1893–95	Corner towers for the office building for the *Glasgow Herald*
1895–96	Martyrs' Public School, Glasgow
1897–98	Interior for the Argyle Street Tearooms, Glasgow (also 1906)
1897–99	Glasgow School of Art (also 1907–09)
1900	Interior at the eighth exhibition of the Vienna Secession (in cooperation with the other members of the Glasgow Four: Ingram Street Tearooms, Glasgow (also 1907, 1909 and 1910–11)
1901	Design for a "House of an Art Lover" competition, organized by a journal of interior design
1902	Interior for the Scottish section of the International Exhibition of Modern Decorative Art in Turin, Italy
1902–05	Hill House, Helensburgh
1903–04	Willow Tearooms, Glasgow (also 1917)
1903–06	Scotland Street School, Glasgow
1916–19	Rebuilding and refurnishing of the house at 78 Derngate, Northampton, England
1923–27	Lives in Port-Vendres, France, where he concentrates on landscape painting
1928	Dies on December 10 in London

The strikingly rectilinear form and extended ladder back of the Glaswegian architect and designer Charles Rennie Mackintosh's chair mark it out as one of the lasting images of design from the first years of the twentieth century. Its reductive simplicity renders it timeless in many ways, and yet it belongs unequivocally to this period when a number of young architects and designers in Britain, Europe and the United States were striving to move beyond the historicism and stylistic eclecticism of the previous century.

Mackintosh designed this ladder-back chair for the Hill House, Helensburgh (Scotland), one of his greatest architectural achievements. The house was built between 1902 and 1905 for the publisher Walter Blackie, and Mackintosh provided extensive furnishings for it in the years 1904–08. While it is tempting to view the chair simply as an abstract, geometric sculpture—one that contradicts the natural, organic tendencies of wood (in this case ebonized to hide the grain) by compressing it into a rigid, unnatural format—it should not be forgotten that the chair was conceived as an element within a complete interior, in this case a soft-white bedroom. For Mackintosh, interiors were to be looked upon as *Gesamtkunstwerk* (complete works of art).

Set in the space for which it was intended, this ladder-back chair can be seen as a formal counterpart to the all-white setting made up of a bed set into a barrelled vault, pieces of fitted furniture and a few free-standing pieces, all painted creamy white. Conscious of the gendered implications of colour and of different domestic spaces, this was the first time that Mackintosh had injected a "masculine" element into a predominantly "feminine" space. The bedroom had soft pink and green stylized rose patterns stencilled onto the walls; the walls themselves and the carpets were also a cream colour.

The chair, one of a pair in the room and probably intended to have clothes placed on it rather than to be sat upon, has a high ladder back surmounted by a wooden grid. The ladder extends to the floor, and the seat, which fans outwards, is minimally upholstered with a light-coloured fabric. The grid at the top echoed others in the Hill House bedroom and an extensive use of the square motif which appeared in stencil form and as cut-outs on other furniture pieces in the room, the bed among them. Its function was primarily one of articulating space. In 1903–04 Mackintosh was moving away from the curved forms of his earlier designs towards a more Japanese-inspired geometry. This shift in emphasis was also prevalent in contemporary Viennese design. P. S.

The black-stained chairs were designed to starkly contrast with the all-white bedroom interior.

Mackintosh's exterior design for the Hill House, 1902–05.

Mass-produced version of the Hill House chair, currently manufactured by Cassina.

RALEIGH SAFETY BICYCLE

The first generation of safety bicycles appeared in the 1870s, laying a strong foundation for the cycling boom of the mid-1890s which involved people across the social spectrum. The Raleigh Cycle Company, Nottingham, England, was one of the firms which was well equipped to cope with this increase in demand, since it had been committed to large-scale bicycle production since its inception in 1889. By the turn of the century it employed more than 350 workers in what was the largest British cycle factory.

The Raleigh Safety Bicycle incorporated fresh modes of construction pioneered by the company in 1900, thus helping to forge a reputation for high quality and lightness. They involved the replacement of machined castings in heavy iron by lighter, stronger steel stampings for the lugs and brackets which held the bicycle frame together, as well as a revolutionary brazing system for strengthening the joints of the frame by dipping it in molten metal. Significantly faster than conventional bicycle manufacturing practices for jointing, which were usually carried out by a blowtorch, the end result was also stronger and lighter than that of Raleigh's principal competitors.

The Raleigh Safety Bicycle set high standards of design, safety and convenience for consumers. Like a number of other safety cycles on the market, the Raleigh was of high quality and boasted stirrup brakes, pneumatic tyres and gears, the last allowing the rider to attack hills with greater ease, as well as achieve greater speeds. In fact, it also incorporated the Sturmey-Archer three-speed hub-gear—patented in 1902 and marketed from 1903—which became the standard prototype for most subsequent gears. Actually manufactured by the Raleigh Cycle Company itself, it attained sales of about 100,000 per year by 1913. To add to the pleasure and convenience of use, a range of accessories was available, including chain cases, tool bags, travel bags, bells, lights and pumps.

Marketing was aided considerably as a result of Raleigh's success in cycle racing, a sport in which the company participated in a number of countries, including France, Italy and Austria. Important in enhancing the international appeal for Raleigh was the American cyclist Arthur Augustus Zimmerman, the most celebrated Raleigh racing cyclist of the turn of the century. He also lent his name to the endorsement of a wide variety of bicycle accessories.

J. M.W.

Quality and safety were utmost in the development of the Safety Bicycles.

Since 1998 Wittman has manufactured a re-edition of the chair with an adjustable backrest.

(inset)
A footrest, hidden beneath the seat, changes the Sitting Machine into a chaise longue.

The architect and designer Josef Hoffmann was one of the pioneers of functional design. In 1897, he helped to found the exhibition group, the Vienna Secession. His fellow exhibitors, the British architects and designers Charles Rennie Mackintosh and Charles Robert Ashbee, significantly influenced the development of Hoffmann's work, which spans the transition from Art Nouveau to the new aesthetic of the machine age. Ashbee's Guild of Handicraft inspired Hoffmann to co-found the Wiener Werkstätte (Viennese Workshops) in 1903 with Koloman Moser and the arts patron Fritz Wärndorfer. These craft workshops manufactured Hoffmann's metalwork and jewellery designs.

One of Hoffmann's most important house designs was for the Palais Stoclet, Brussels (1905–11), which exemplified his geometric aesthetic. Hoffmann exercised absolute control over its interiors, for which he designed furniture made by the Wiener Werkstätte. Like the Viennese architects Adolf Loos and Otto Wagner, Hoffmann also designed furniture for Thonet, famous for their bentwood furniture. Pre-1914, this company dominated the Austro-German furniture market, employing more than 6,000 workers and producing annually 2 million pieces of furniture which were exported worldwide.

Hoffmann's *Sitzmaschine* (Sitting Machine), made by Thonet, was first shown at the Vienna Kunstschau in 1908. It could be made entirely by machine, as the chair was produced from ebonized wood, without any upholstery. The central back splat, contained within a tubular frame, is pierced by a grid of two rows of square holes. The back is adjustable and held in place by a rod which pierces a series of knobs fixed into the arms. The latter extend to form curving frames around the chair's side panels. Each panel is perforated with two grids: vertical slots above and a single tower of square cells below. The plain wooden seat of the chair rests on two ball finials at the front. These motifs had already started to appear in Hoffmann's work from 1904, for example, the ebonized beech and plywood chair, with red oilcloth seat, designed for the dining hall of the Purkersdorf Sanatorium.

Hoffmann tended to work intuitively, concentrating on design and visual treatment and relying on technical assistants in his office to work on precise drawings and specifications. Hoffmann remained active throughout his life. One year before his death, he produced preliminary designs for a town hall in Addis Ababa, Ethiopia, with glass façades. His design work underwent a rediscovery in the 1980s, with some of his furniture being reproduced under licence.   D.B.

Josef Hoffmann

1870   Born on December 15 in Pirnitz, Moravia
1887   Begins attending the Imperial and Royal State Technical School, Brünn (now Brno, Czech Republic), at the same time as Adolf Loos
1892–95 Studies architecture at the Academy of Fine Arts, Vienna, with Karl von Hasenauer and, as of 1894, Otto Wagner
1897   Co-founder of the Vienna Secession, for which he designs numerous exhibitions
1899   Begins teaching at the School for Arts and Crafts (today the School for the Applied Arts) in Vienna
1900–02 Housing complex for Koloman Moser, Carl Moll, Hugo Henneberg and Friedrich Viktor Spitzer on the Hohe Warte in Vienna
1903   Founds the Wiener Werkstätte with the industrialist Fritz Wärndorfer and Koloman Moser; artistic director until 1931
1904–05 Purkersdorf Sanatorium, near Vienna (including interior design)
1905   Leaves the Vienna Secession
1905–11 Palais Stoclet, Brussels (including interior design)
1908   Architectural master plan and design of the entrance building for the Kunstschau, Vienna
1912   Founds the Austrian Werkbund and heads it until 1920
1914   Austrian Pavilion at the Werkbund exhibition in Cologne
1924–25 Austrian Pavilion at the International Exhibition of Arts and Crafts in Paris
1934   Austrian Pavilion for the Venice Biennale
1956   Dies on May 7 in Vienna

Hoffmann used the perforated surface as early as 1904 in a chair designed for the dining hall at Purkersdorf Sanatorium.

FORD MODEL T

Henry Ford

Henry Ford

1863	Born on July 30 in Greenfield Township, Michigan
1879–82	Works as an apprentice in a machine shop in Detroit
1891–99	Employed as an engineer for the Edison Illuminating Company in Detroit
1896	Builds the "Quadricycle," his first car
1903	After two failed attempts to set up a motor car factory, founds the Ford Motor Company in Detroit; puts his first Model A on the market
1908	Introduces the Model T
1910	Opens a factory in Highland Park, Michigan, which from 1913 onwards uses assembly-line production methods
1917	Begins construction of a factory beside the River Rouge in Dearborn, Michigan
1919	His son Edsel is appointed chairman of the board of Ford
1926	Introduces the Ford "Tri-Motor" aircraft
1927	All production facilities are concentrated at the River Rouge factory; production of the Model T ceases; the New Model A is put on the market
1932	Introduction of the Ford V-8 engine
1947	Dies on April 7 in Dearborn

On December 19, 1999, the Ford Model T was named "Car of the Century" by the Car of the Century International Jury, thus securing Henry Ford's prominence as a great industrial innovator. The Model T was the first fully completed in-house construction at the Ford Motor Company, founded in 1903 in Detroit, intended to popularize the automobile. And it more than achieved this goal. Ford explained, "The greatest demand today is for an inexpensive car with a sufficiently powerful motor, manufactured from the best material.... It must be strong enough for American roads and capable of driving wherever horse-drawn carriages are able to pass without the driver having to fear for his car." The Model T had a four-cylinder engine, two gears for accelerating, one for reversing (the driver used a foot pedal to change gears) and, in the beginning, only a cloth top without side panels. In 1908, the first demonstration model caused a sensation and became an overnight success with the public. To meet the high demand, in 1910 Ford commissioned industrial architect Albert Kahn (1869–1942) to build a spacious new factory in Highland Park, near Detroit, Michigan.

The prerequisite for mass production was precision in all the manufactured parts; to this end Ford developed many tools and machines himself. Yet the Model T was not manufactured on an assembly line from the start. Assembly-line production began only in 1913 in response to the ever-increasing demand. In previous years the cars were assembled by groups of workers on site, but now the workers stood at a moving band on which the parts rolled past them. The manufacturing process as a whole was increasingly driven by the uninterrupted flow of materials and components. Ford and his chief engineers Sorensen and Martin ran empirical tests of this revolutionary new approach, rehearsed it and then implemented it in one production area after another. This brought about a dramatic increase in production, coupled with a steady decrease in price. In 1909, some 14,000 cars were manufactured, but by 1916 the number had risen to 585,000; the sales price dropped from $950 to $360 over the same period. Ford's position was strong enough to offer his car in only one colour—black—for many years. He resisted working on aesthetic considerations.

With unusual generosity Ford published detailed descriptions and drawings of his plant installations. Over time, nearly all parts of the car were modified, although the changes were technical rather than stylistic. The year 1921 was a record one: 55 per cent of all American cars were Ford's Model T. But by 1926 the market share had dropped to 30 per cent. The Ford Motor Company now faced stiff competition from General Motors, whose design department was called Art and Color Studios and whose policy of creating new models every year with an emphasis on style and aesthetics was a great success with the public. Design had become an optical bonus value. In 1927, after producing 15 million Model Ts, production ceased abruptly, and a more modern successor was developed virtually overnight—the new Model A. Even today, the Model T exemplifies the dramatic impact of design on automobile and industrial production.   C.L.

(above)
The Model T Cabriolet from
1914 had only a canvas top
without side panels.

(from left to right)
Model T Cabriolet, 1914
Model T Coupé, 1917–19
Model T Touring Car, 1913

AEG ELECTRIC KETTLE
Peter Behrens

Peter Behrens

1868	Born on April 14 in Hamburg
1886–91	Studies successively at the School for Arts and Crafts in Hamburg, the Art School in Karlsruhe and the Düsseldorf Academy
1892	Co-founder of the Munich Secession
1897	Co-founder of the Vereinigte Werkstätten für Kunst im Handwerk (Association of Decorative Art Workshops), Munich
1900	Designs exterior and interior of his own house on the Mathildenhöhe, Darmstadt
1902	Participates in the "International Exhibition of Modern Decorative Art" in Turin, Italy
1904–05	Hall of the Folkwang Museum, Hagen; designs extension to the living room of the Haus Schede, Wetter
1905–06	Crematorium, Delstern
1907–14	Appointed artistic director to AEG; designs buildings, products and publicity material for the company
1908–11	His firm employs Walter Gropius (1908–10), Ludwig Mies van der Rohe (1908–11) and Le Corbusier (1910)
1909	AEG turbine factory, Berlin
1920–24	Head office for IG-Farben, Hoechst
1927	Terrace house on the Weissenhof housing complex, Stuttgart
1940	Dies on February 27 in Berlin

1907 marks a milestone in the history of design: in June 1907 Peter Behrens was appointed artistic director to AEG (Allgemeine Elektricitäts-Gesellschaft) in Berlin and shortly afterwards—in October—the Deutscher Werkbund was founded in Munich. Behrens was the common factor in both events. He was one of the founding members of the Werkbund and his work for AEG was seen by many as the realization of the association's ideals. Never before had a designer had as great an influence on a large industrial enterprise as Behrens. He alone was responsible for all aspects relating to the visual image of AEG—Behrens developed their first corporate identity—from the graphic design of the company's stationery to a full range of products, as well as architecture. The highlight of his architectural contributions was the construction of the Berlin turbine factory in 1909.

Engineer Michael von Dolivo-Dobrovolsky provided the technological prerequisites in his approach to optimizing mass production by no longer concentrating on individual products but on the manufacture of standardized components that could be used for a whole range of different appliances. The electric kettles from 1909 are a perfect example of the collaboration between technician von Dolivo-Dobrovolsky, who had little interest in the external form of the product, and designer Behrens. Behrens designed three different basic shapes—cylindrical, semi-oval, octagonal—available in three sizes: .75 , 1.25 , 1.75 litres. All kettles were produced in brass or copper. Since the brass kettles were also offered in a nickel-plated version, the model was available in three different metal surfaces, which were moreover sold in a chased (flocked or striped) or smooth finish. This resulted in a total of 81 optional combinations, of which only 30 were produced in the end. Standardized patterns were developed for the individual components such as buttons, handles, plugs and heating elements.

In his design, Behrens aimed to do justice to the innovative construction and machine manufacture of these appliances: electric kettles were as much innovations of the electrical industry in its infancy as were fans, turbines, power aggregates or clocks. He avoided formal and decorative allusions to handmade antecedents by reducing form and ornament to the absolute minimum. In doing so, Behrens liberated these electric appliances from their association with expensive, exclusive use and their typical ornamentation as handcrafted, one-of-a-kind pieces. The electric kettles, but also other electric appliances, were intended as products for mass consumption that would find their way into all households. However, the price tag still proved too high for most people, and the goals of the Deutscher Werkbund—educating the masses in good taste by means of well-designed objects offered at moderate prices—was realized only to a limited degree. J.St.

(far right)
AEG catalogue leaflet for electric tea and water kettles, 1910.

Design to a minimum: Behrens intended this elegant water kettle to set new standards over earlier, hand-crafted designs.

An innovation for housewives: AEG advertisement for an electric water kettle, ca. 1910.

LEICA CAMERA
Oskar Barnack

Oskar Barnack

1879	Born on November 1 in Lynow, near Luckenwalde, Germany
	Trains as a mechanic in Berlin, followed by journeyman's travel years
1911	Begins work as a master mechanic for the firm Ernst Leitz, Wetzlar
1913	Develops a small-format camera (24 x 36 mm), the first Leica
1918	"Leica A" developed from the first Leica
1925	Start of Leica production series
1936	Dies on January 16 in Bad Nauheim

Oskar Barnack in his workshop.

The Leica camera was created by precision engineer Oskar Barnack, head of the research department at the Leitz laboratories in Wetzlar, Germany. Barnack developed the camera in 1913 as a private endeavour. At the time, Leitz manufactured mostly microscopes. Barnack suffered from asthma and set himself the task of constructing a lightweight camera to avoid the awkwardness of working with a tripod and 13-by-18-centimetre glass plates. Based on the resolution capacity of the human eye, he arrived at a minimum negative-image size of 24 by 36 millimetres, a mere fraction of the glass-plate format. The only film material with a sufficiently fine grain available at that time was motion-picture film. Barnack's decision to use motion-picture-film format—and thus negatives on a spool instead of a plate—was the first groundbreaking step towards the evolution of the small-format camera. The only difference between film for motion-picture cameras and film for (still) cameras lay in the orientation of the negative on the spool, which was horizontal in the latter.

In 1913, Barnack built two unnamed Leica models, which he kept for many years for personal use. Much later, when economic consolidation occurred in 1925, Leitz introduced this masterpiece of conception and precision, quaintly named Leica (Leitz Camera), to the market: it was an immediate success and sales were correspondingly high. The main principles of the modern camera sprang from this model. Since the filmstrip was protected inside a cartridge from exposure to light, film could easily be changed in daylight. In the Leica, shutter action and film transport were coupled from the very beginning. With a capacity of 36 negatives per film, fabulous optics and precision mechanics (focal plane shutter, retractable lens and, later, interchangeable lenses), the camera set standards that endure to this day.

The Leica made photography mobile. Handheld shots became possible, and the image could be vertical or horizontal in the frame. The 7-centimetre-high, 13-centimetre-wide body of the camera is designed to be held in front of the eye while the user presses the trigger at the same time (no cable trigger). The outstandingly sharp coated lens allowed for enlargements in which the grain of the film material could not be suppressed but instead became an active means of expression. At the Bauhaus in Dessau, artist Herbert Bayer experimented with his new Leica in 1927 by taking photographs while riding a bicycle. It is no exaggeration to say that photojournalism has been defined by the Leica.

This model is the ancestor of all small-format cameras and, although it is a "mere" high-calibre viewfinder camera, it is the source of the configuration used in reflex-type cameras, which are today manufactured predominantly in the Far East. The enduring reputation of the Leica has played a considerable role in ensuring Leitz's position as the manufacturer of the Leicaflex to this day. C.L.

The Leica prototype was used to test the new technology.

Masterfully designed and
technologically innovative,
the Leica made photography
accessible to everyone.

Advertisement for Coca-Cola, 1933.

John Stith Pemberton, a respected pharmacist in Atlanta, Georgia, was a creative man. Like other professional pharmacists of his day, many of whom came close to quackery, he created his own secret recipes to cure his ailing customers. His first concoction was a cough syrup, "Globe of Flower," which was not a great hit. His next invention was "Extract of Stylinger," which again failed to bring him the success he dreamed of; even his "French Wine of Coca" failed to achieve much of a market. Clients kept complaining that all his preparations tasted horrible.

On May 8, 1886, however, in the same year that the Statue of Liberty, that other great American symbol, was erected, Pemberton brewed a new variation over an open fire in his backyard that—after a slow start—would change the world. Only after he had diluted his dark syrup with soda water were some customers of Jacob's Pharmacy willing to give this new drink a try. In the first year, only about 3,200 glasses were sold, either as medicine or as refreshment. Even the suggestion that the drink might increase the drinker's potency had little effect on sales. His business partner, Frank Robinson, thought up the name Coca-Cola and was also responsible for the graceful lettering which has been used ever since, virtually unchanged, as the brand name and trademark.

Some years later, after Pemberton's death, the rights were sold to Asa Candler, who set up the Coca-Cola Company in Atlanta in 1892. The syrup was delivered to popular soda fountains in the district and was diluted with soda water in the customer's glass. In 1894, a number of bottlers obtained the right to fill bottles with a combination of the syrup and soda water on condition that the syrup could only be prepared by the Coca-Cola Company, which would continue to be responsible for all advertising. This system of franchising is still in use.

The independent bottlers used their own bottles so that, as the number of bottlers increased and distribution gradually extended more widely across the United States, the drink began to be delivered in bottles of all sorts of different shapes and sizes, making things very easy for imitators. Even the brand name seemed to provide insufficient protection. The company regularly found itself involved in lawsuits to protect its product, and the different bottles made it more and more difficult to produce good advertising. In 1915, the problem was solved by the company designing its own bottle. A competition was held, and it was won by the Root Glass Company. Their office assistant, sent to the library to find an illustration of a cola nut to be used as a model for the design, returned with a picture of a cocoa pod torn from an encyclopaedia. Nobody knows who thought up the design. In 1915, the patent was registered in the name of the manager, Alexander Samuelson. In 1916, a slimmer version of the bottle came into production, and it is this version, coupled with the brand name and the trademark, that has made the image of Coca-Cola.   R.K.

Coca-Cola is at home anywhere. This bottle originates from the People's Republic of China.

The evolution of the Coca-Cola bottle: from the unlabelled bottle of 1915 to its characteristic size and shape of today.

U.S. "TUNNEL" MAILBOX

Roy Joroleman

Simple and functional: the deep tunnel shape is ideal for mail and newspapers, while the raised flag indicates the arrival of new mail.

The design of the "tunnel" mailbox grew out of an ongoing attempt by the U.S. Postal Service to standardize mail delivery on rural routes. With the advent of Rural Free Delivery of U.S. Mail to farmers in 1896, letter carriers faced a gamut of discarded containers serving as mailboxes, ranging from lard cans to feed boxes—some with traces of their original contents. The Post Office deplored this form of adaptive re-use and decided to rectify matters.

As James H. Bruns, National Postal Museum Director, tells the story, in 1901 the Postal Service gathered a committee to determine mailbox specifications and review 63 designs submitted by prospective manufacturers. The guidelines directed that boxes were to be made of sheet metal, preferably galvanized and should have an adjustable and durable sign that would signal the presence of mail. The committee gave its approval to mailboxes from 14 manufacturers. Use of these boxes was mandated, for "unless the boxes built on new routes are of approved patterns, they will not be served by rural carriers."

Bruns explains that this edict often put letter carriers in the middle of a conflict between fiercely independent farmers and government regulators. Furthermore, the boxes, designed for letters, were not large enough to accommodate parcels. In response to these problems, another postal committee was convened in 1915 to search for a new solution, based on models already in production and new designs submitted by manufacturers. Still, none of these were approved. Instead, Bruns relates, the government turned to Roy Joroleman, a postal engineer, to resolve matters. His design for a tunnel-shaped metal mailbox with a flag to signal the letter carrier to pick up mail (or the owner to collect mail) has been cited as an ideal combination of simplicity and functionality. To encourage competition among manufacturers, Joroleman's now-famous design was not allowed to be patented. A larger version of his design, known as the "No. 2 Size Box," was approved in 1928 to accommodate both letters and parcels.

Over succeeding decades, that farmer's mailbox could be found in American suburbs. Its simple shape, together with raised flag, was a nostalgic symbol for many of the new semi-city dwellers who had grown up in the countryside.

Today, this very same mailbox design can be found around the world—but only two-dimensionally, on computer screens. This box is the iconic symbol used to mark the arrival and sending of e-mail via the Internet, making it an international symbol of news and information at the close of the century. As well put by Bruns: Joroleman's box "represents mail for a lot of people."   J.S.

To spare the postal worker a long walk up the driveway, clusters of mailboxes are often found by the roadside in many rural areas.

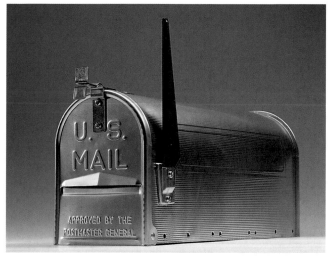

Dutch designers have always shown a preference for simple materials and clear-cut constructions, whether in jewellery or furniture. Expensive types of wood, precious metals and gems have always been used, at the most, as additional details. The important aspect has always been the expression of a form, not the "status" of the production material. From their perspective, a perfect piece of jewellery can just as easily be made from paper, or a chair from pine. Dutch designers choose certain materials because they express particular qualities. The work produced by the furniture-maker and architect Gerrit Rietveld is replete with these characteristics, of which two of his designs provide the absolute synthesis: the "Red-Blue" armchair and the house that he designed in 1924 in collaboration with Truus Schröder.

The first versions of the Red-Blue armchair were created somewhere around 1917, at a time when Rietveld had only recently opened his own furniture workshop. The chair was stained black; there was one version for men and a smaller version for women. Rietveld's intent was to design a piece of furniture that could be cheaply mass-produced. As with many of his designs, he used standard beechwood laths and thin pine planks, the sort of things that can be bought from any timber merchant. A special characteristic of many of his chairs is that the intersections where the laths cross one another are fixed by wooden pegs. The functions of construction, the seat, the back and armrests, are explicitly separated from one another visually. Rietveld, in fact, saw the chair as the skeleton of an overstuffed armchair from which all unnecessary additions had been removed. His aim—as he put it himself—was to make a piece of furniture with neither volume nor mass, a piece which did not enclose space but left it undisturbed.

In 1917, Theo van Doesburg (1883–1931) founded De Stijl (The Style), a movement in which artists, architects and designers strove to achieve a new visual culture. In 1919, in the periodical of the same name, van Doesburg recorded a description of the chair, which at the time was still black. Although Rietveld felt a certain kinship with the work of the Dutch painter Piet Mondrian (1872–1944) and the architects J.J. Pieter Oud (1890–1963) and Mart Stam (1899–1986), he always remained on the fringes of the movement.

It was only in about 1923 that the black chair was given the colours so characteristic of De Stijl's emphasis on colour. It has often been suggested that the chair was based on a rigid system of sizing. But Rietveld was never as strict as that. He was much more concerned with the visual impression created by a system than with any dogmatic approach. Thus, his chairs could be made of turned pieces of wood and produced in a variety of sizes and colours, including pink, green, white and grey.   R.K.

Gerrit Rietveld

The Red-Blue armchair's now characteristic colour scheme was not devised until 1923.

(right)
The Red-Blue armchair was used as a decorative element in the interior design of the Rietveld-Schröder House, 1923–24.

TABLE LAMP
Wilhelm Wagenfeld and Carl Jacob Jucker

Wilhelm Wagenfeld   Carl Jacob Jucker

Wilhelm Wagenfeld

1900	Born on April 15 in Bremen, Germany
1914–18	Apprentices as a draughtsman at Koch & Bergfeld silverware factory, Bremen
1916–19	Attends the School for Arts and Crafts, Bremen
1919–22	Attends the State Drawing Academy, Main
1923–25	Trains in the metal workshop at the Bauhaus, Weimar; journeyman examination as silversmith and engraver in 1924
1926	Assistant in the metal workshop at the State School for Architecture, Weimar
1930	Self-employed; collaboration with the Ottmar Zieher jewellery factory, Schwäbisch Gmünd
1931	Begins work in the Schott & Gen. Glass Workshops in Jena, Germany
1931–35	Professor at the State Academy of Fine Arts, Berlin
1935	Artistic director of the United Glass Workshops of Lausitz, Weisswasser, Saxony
1946	Helps found the School for Applied Arts, Dresden
1947–49	Head of the Standardization and Norms Department at the Institute for Civil Engineering of the German Academy of Sciences, Berlin; Professor of Industrial Design at the School of Fine Arts, Berlin
1950	Works exclusively on a self-employed basis in industry, including for WMF, Geislingen (until 1977)
1954	Founds the Wagenfeld Workshop
1978	Closes his workshop and retires
1990	Dies on May 28 in Stuttgart

Carl Jacob Jucker

1902	Born on August 22 in Zurich, Switzerland
1918–22	Trains as a silversmith at the School for Arts and Crafts, Zurich
1922	Studies at the Bauhaus; foundation course with Georg Muche; works in the metal workshop under Christian Dell
1923	Design of lighting fixtures for the Musterhaus am Horn
1924	Designer for the Jezler & Cie. AG silverware factory, Schaffhausen; teacher at the Professional School for Applied and Industrial Arts, Schaffhausen
1997	Dies in Schaffhausen

One of the many material-oriented workshops at the Bauhaus focused on metal. Beginning in 1923 this workshop was led by the Hungarian artist László Moholy-Nagy (1895–1946). Among other things, he set the contemporary standards for lighting design, including, and indeed using, glass as a material. In 1923, Carl Jacob Jucker was the first at the Bauhaus to develop a table lamp with a glass base and spindle, making the electricity supply visible by virtue of the cord. The lampshade, however, was still a metal reflector. Then, in 1924, Wilhelm Wagenfeld developed a metal lamp with a nickel spindle, metal base and a dome-shaped lampshade made of frosted glass, analogous to the existing Jucker lamps. That same year—once again inspired by Moholy-Nagy—Wagenfeld created a version completely in glass, including the base and spindle. In keeping with the "building kit" mentality prevalent in many of the Bauhaus workshops, he combined available parts from the glass and metal versions into new and varied combinations in order to reach optimal results.

Despite the use of many prefabricated products, and in the face of the lamp's seemingly technological air, today the lamp can only be manufactured with a high degree of manual craftsmanship, making it more expensive than mass-produced industrial lamps. Nonetheless, the lamp reigns as one of the archetypal images of the pure, simple form and elementary design promoted by the Bauhaus. It also reflects the symbiosis of art and technology proscribed and promoted by Walter Gropius (1883–1969), the founder of the Bauhaus in Weimar, while serving as a prototype for industrial production. The individual elements of the lamp are aesthetically weighed out: bearing and loading, floating and containing, in balance. This is in no small way attributable to the lamp's link to designs by Adolf Loos (1870–1933) and Josef Hoffmann in the Wiener Werkstätte, although Wagenfeld chose a cooler, more modern sentiment by changing materials from brass to nickel. Hence, the frosted-glass shade, for example, as well as its attachment to a narrow metal ring with three knurled screws, is not uncommon at the turn of the century.

Beginning in 1930, when the Bauhaus lamps were produced by varying licensees instead of the school's workshops, the pure half-circle of the frosted-glass lampshade became the five-eighths circle common up to our day. Only in 1980 did the Tecnolumen Company in Bremen—after two decades of aesthetically unsatisfying plagiarism—issue re-editions of both lamp variations in collaboration with Wagenfeld. This reduced the total volume by about one-tenth, in order to lend the lamp more agreeable dimensions. Seen at the time of conception as a rather cold and unpleasant design, since the boom in the 1980s of the so-called Modern Classic, the lamps—as well as the steel pipe furniture from Marcel Breuer, Ludwig Mies van der Rohe, Eileen Gray or Le Corbusier (see pp. 39, 45, 46, 48)—have come to be accepted as archetypes of the Bauhaus aesthetic. Firstly, by virtue of the symbolic form of the overstretched frosted-glass lampshade, reminding one of the gentle luminance of the moon and thus enriching the lamp's technical aspiration with poetic associations. Secondly, the subtle way in which the light emanates—not only light from the light bulb but also the discretely functional lampshade as well—reflects an archetypal nature. Thus, this Bauhaus lamp succeeds in bridging the apparent contradiction between technical pretension and a notion of beauty oriented towards warmer, more traditional images.   V. F.

From the Bauhaus's "Catalogue of Patterns."

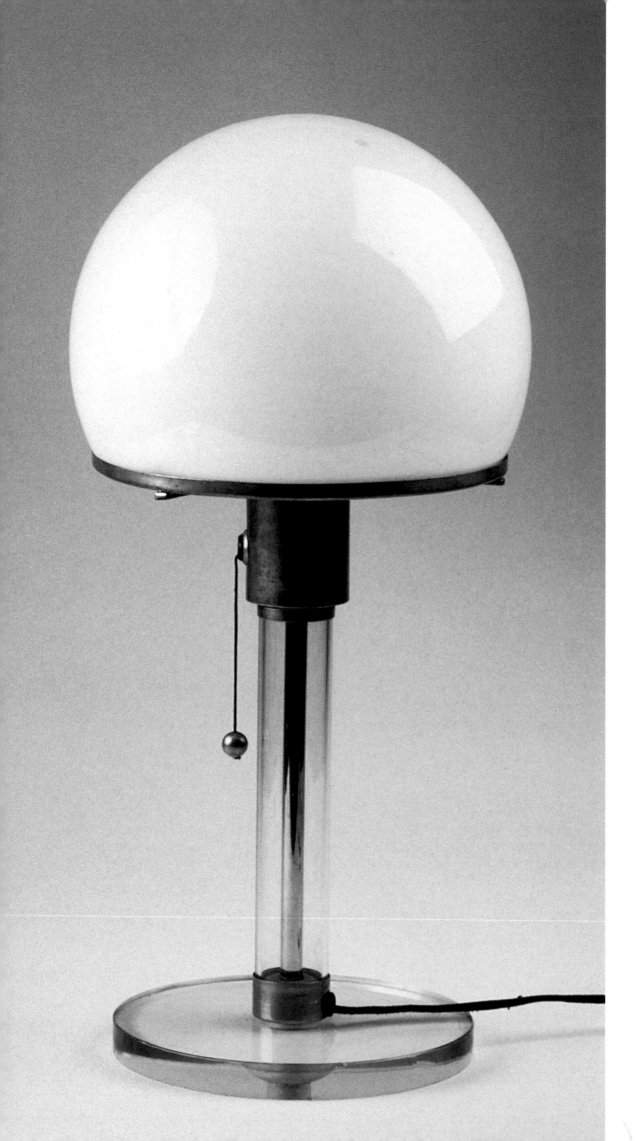

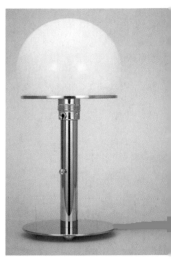

Re-edition with metal base
by Tecnolumen.

Original edition
with glass base,
1923.

Marcel Breuer's design for the
study at the Grote house with
Wagenfeld's table lamp,
Dessau, 1927.

TEASET

Marianne Brandt

Made in brass and silver plate with ebony handles, this teaset typified the more progressive trends in design at the Bauhaus in Weimar. Essentially exploring the interrelationship of basic geometric forms, it had much in common with a number of avant-garde movements of the day, including Constructivism and De Stijl. Such a progressive outlook took root at the Bauhaus from 1923 when a new slogan—"Art and Technology: A New Unity"—was adopted by its influential founding director, Walter Gropius. The manipulation of elemental forms could also be found in other design fields at the Bauhaus. These included typography, where Josef Albers's (1888–1976) stencilled letterforms of the mid-1920s were based on the manipulation of three, basic, geometric shapes, and furniture, where Marcel Breuer's exploration of simple elements in his cantilever chair presented a thoroughly modern solution to the problem of seating. Brandt's teaset design is characteristic of the early phases of modernism, a concept which gathered pace in a number of European countries as the 1920s unfolded. Form predominates over ornament and there is a strong sense of contemporaneity in the manipulation of abstract form combined with a sense of "form follows function" and a clear sense of (at least symbolic) compatibility with modern mass-production technology.

Interestingly, as recent research has revealed, Marianne Brandt (like the furniture designer Alma Büscher) was one of a few exceptions at the Bauhaus to figure prominently in design fields outside arts and crafts practices generally associated with women, such as those of weaving, pottery or bookbinding. Indeed, from 1920 onwards Gropius had sought to introduce a more rigorous policy for admission to the Bauhaus, "particularly for the female sex whose number is excessive." Such circumstances notwithstanding, Brandt was clearly influenced by Gropius's "Art and Technology" rallying-call in her exploration of the aesthetic possibilities of the modernist *Zeitgeist* which was to dominate the Bauhaus in the later half of the 1920s, particularly after its move to Dessau in 1925. Brandt worked under the Hungarian Constructivist László Moholy-Nagy who had arrived at the Bauhaus in Weimar as head of the metal workshop in 1923. He also became a key figure in the foundation course where students learnt to explore materials and the principles of construction. However, in common with many other Bauhaus designs of the time, Brandt's 1924 teaset is still essentially handmade, albeit a prototype for industrial production. A number of her later designs for lighting and other products were subsequently put into mass production by firms such as Körting & Mathiessen of Leipzig.

Recognition of Brandt as a leading figure of German modernism has been confirmed by the reproduction in 1985, by the fashionable Italian metalware design company Alessi, of an ashtray designed by her in 1926. J. M.W.

Marianne Brandt

1893	Born Marianne Liebe on October 6 in Chemnitz, Germany
1911–17	Studies painting and sculpture at the Royal Saxon Academy for the Fine Arts
1917–23	Works as a freelance artist
1924	Attends the *Vorkurs* (foundation course) given by Josef Albers and László Moholy-Nagy at the Bauhaus, Weimar
1925–26	Trainee in the machine shop run by the Bauhaus (from 1925 in Dessau); during this period mainly designs metal objects for domestic use
1927–29	Deputy manager of the machine shop; concerns herself primarily with designing light fittings for various companies
1929	Bauhaus diploma; employed briefly by Walter Gropius's firm in Berlin
1930–33	Artistic assistant at the metalware factory Ruppelwerk, Gotha
1933–49	Works as a freelance artist
1949–54	Employed as a teacher at the State School for Applied Arts, Dresden and the School for the Applied Arts, Berlin-Weissensee
1983	Dies on June 18 in Kirchberg, Saxony

Original 1924 teaset by Brandt.
In 1985, the Bauhaus Archives,
Berlin, granted reproduction rights
for Brandt's teaset to Alessi.

Reproduction of an
ashtray design by Brandt,
1926; today manufactured
by Alessi, 1985.

Walter Gropius's living
room, Bauhaus campus,
Dessau, 1926–27.

Marcel Breuer distinguished himself early on as an exceptionally talented apprentice in the cabinet-maker's workshop at the Bauhaus in Weimar. There he worked with wood and cloth from the Bauhaus weaving mill. The chairs created by Breuer from these materials in Weimar between 1922 and 1925—most remained one-of-a-kind pieces—have become highly sought-after and valuable collectables.

The Bauhaus was forced to move to Dessau in 1925 because of the political climate. The change in geography brought with it a change in the institution's direction. In the quiet and sheltered atmosphere of Weimar, industry had been an intellectual source of inspiration rather than a concrete basis for production. But in Dessau, the home of the Junker airplane factory, state-of-the-art industry was literally on the school's doorstep.

With the first tubular-steel chair (only later named after the Russian painter Wassily Kandinsky, 1866–1944), Breuer took a giant step towards industrial product design. He incorporated the De Stijl's design principles, which fascinated him, with new materials and forms of construction—from wooden strut-and-panel construction to tubular steel, or cloth-covered areas stretched between the frame. As legend has it, Breuer was inspired to use bent tubular steel in furniture design while riding his bicycle and looking down at the handlebar. This chair was Breuer's first attempt with standard-strength tubular steel (three-quarter inch Mannesmann tubes).

Although the design was realized off-site—the Bauhaus facilities were probably not equipped to handle the heating and bending of tubular steel—it is a visual representation of the curriculum at the Bauhaus in Dessau under the directorship of Walter Gropius. The newly inaugurated Bauhaus building contained, among other things, a famous photograph of the "masked woman" in this chair for a press release at the end of 1926.

The first prototype still lacked the runners which were to be characteristic of later models; instead, it stood on feet linked by a low crossbeam. The individual components of the chair (seat, back, armrests and feet) were axially welded. From the very beginning, the design included criss-crossed textile areas. Hannes Meyer published an image of this early version with his text "The New World" in the Swiss magazine *Das Werk* (1926). Work continued on the design following a "monolinear principle," and the result was a fascinating structure of laterally bolted elements that were mutually stabilizing. The chairs were easily disassembled, and several could be shipped inside a box; but this was only a side-effect of the design, which went into serial production as a "Bauhaus model." It was manufactured by Standard Möbel (Berlin) and, in a slightly modified version, by Thonet. National Socialism put a stop to production. However, when Bauhaus-type design experienced a glorious revival in the late 1960s, the "Wassily" chair too made a big comeback in a new edition produced by Cassina and Thonet.   C.L.

Marcel Breuer

1902	Born on May 22 in Pécs, Hungary
1920	After briefly studying at the Academy of Fine Arts, Vienna, he enrols at the Bauhaus, Weimar, where he becomes a trainee in the woodworking shop
1922–24	Lath chair "ti 1a"
1923	Furniture maker for the Haus am Horn, Weimar
1925–28	Foreman at the Bauhaus furniture workshop
1925–26	"Wassily" chair
1927	The firm Standard Möbel Berlin begins to put a number of his furniture designs into production; furnishing for the Piscator House, Berlin
1932	Realizes his first architectural work, the Harnischmacher House
1932–34	Works mainly in Switzerland; designs aluminium furniture for Wohnbedarf, Zurich (construction by Embru, Rüti)
1935–37	Works as an architect in London; designs laminated wood furniture for Isokon, London
1937	Emigrates to the United States; lectures at the University of Harvard; joins Walter Gropius in setting up an architectural firm
1947	Designs his own house in New Canaan, Connecticut
1953–58	Head office for UNESCO in Paris (with Pier Luigi Nervi and Bernard Louis Zehrfuss)
1963–66	Designs the Whitney Museum of American Art, New York
1981	Dies on July 1 in New York

Marcel Breuer in his Wassily chair, 1925–26.

ROLEX OYSTER WATCH

The Rolex is designed to handle the most extreme weather conditions—even the top of Mount Everest.

Rolex watches are world famous for the quality of their design and manufacture and for their timekeeping precision. In recent years, they have also acquired a rather more dubious appeal to thieves. In London, for example, a series of robberies from the wealthy have included Rolex thefts. The Rolex "Oyster" watch is one of the wristwatches for which Rolex has become so renowned. First invented in 1926, it is the waterproof watch *par excellence*. Its essential features depend on the sealing together of two layers of metal forming its case. The perfection of this seal means that the watch itself is completely watertight, resulting in its keeping perfect time, even when tested in the most gruelling of conditions.

The first Rolex wristwatch was launched in 1905, offering a more practical contrast to traditional fob or pocket watches, especially for active use. Rolex's trademark was registered in 1908 by Hans Wilsdorf, one of the company's founders. In 1910, the Rolex watch-chronometer won a "First Class Certificate" at Bienne, Switzerland. Work on perfecting accurate timekeeping continued, and, by 1914, these efforts were recognized by London's Kew Observatory, which normally granted awards only to marine chronometers. The award marked the true beginning of Rolex's international reputation.

On October 7, 1927, Rolex made history when Mercedes Gleitz, a London stenographer, wore a Rolex Oyster wristwatch during a cross-Channel swim. She emerged from her ordeal with the watch in perfect running order. Refinements to the basic design followed: in 1931, the Rolex Oyster Perpetual was invented. This was the first self-winding, waterproof watch and the forerunner of all automatic watches. In 1953, Rolex Perpetual chronometers were worn by Sir John Hunt and his team in their ascent of Everest.

Rolex Oyster watches are manufactured in Switzerland under the most stringent quality controls. Each case is made from a solid block of stainless steel, 18 carat gold or platinum and is given a unique serial number. Its crystal is cut from a block of synthetic sapphire, which is extremely hard and virtually scratchproof; its Cyclops lens magnifies the data two-and-a-half times to make it easily visible. According to the type of model, the winding crown is of either twinlock or triplelock construction, conferring maximum protection against dust and water.

Oyster watches are made with either mechanical or quartz movements. The mechanical types have 220 components and are self-winding, with pivotal rotor arms. The quartz examples are engineered to be resistant to magnetic interference of up to 80,000 amplitude modulation. Every Rolex Oyster chronometer is individually tested by the Swiss Chronometers' Control office for 15 days and nights, under the most rigorous conditions. Success means that it receives a red seal and the inscription "Superlative Chronometer Officially Certified," confirming its exceptional reliability and quality. Rolex watches are available worldwide: its "Calendar" watches are consequently made with the days of the week spelt out in full, in any one of 26 languages.   D.B.

The first Oyster was introduced to the market in 1926 and the first watch with fully automated wind-up mechanism in 1931.

(opposite, from left to right)
The Datejust—the first chronometer with automatic date display, 1945.
Oyster Perpetual Air-King
Oyster Perpetual Datejust
Oyster Perpetual Explorer
Oyster Day-Date in gold
Oyster Perpetual in steel

BUGATTI

Ettore Arco Isidoro Bugatti

Ettore Arco Isidoro Bugatti

1881	Born on September 15 in Milan
1897	Apprenticeship at the bicycle factory of Prinetti & Stucchi, Milan
1900–01	First automobile with the aid of Count Gulinelli; gold medal at the Milan Auto Salon
1902–04	Head of the automobile department at De Dietrich, Niederbronn, Alsace
1905	Design of the "Hermes Simplex" automobile for the Elsässische Maschinenbau-Gesellschaft
1907–09	Freelance work for the Gasmotorenfabrik Deutz, Cologne
1910	Type 13 production begins, Molsheim, Alsace
1911–12	Designs for Peugeot ("Bébé" Peugeot), licenses distributed to Germany and England
1914	350 Bugattis are constructed; relocates to Milan and then to Paris
1919	Factory in Molsheim reopened
1921	Race success at the Grand Prix of Italy, Brescia
1923	Construction of an auto body factory, Molsheim
1925	412 race victories in 9 months
1926	Construction of the first Royale Type 41 with 15-litre (!) piston displacement
1931–32	Construction of railroad locomotives with "Royale" motors
1934–40	Production of the Type 57—the best-known automobile; bodywork design from son Jean Bugatti
1938–39	Construction of an airplane and a speed boat
1940	Factory in Molsheim is sold
1947	Dies on August 21 in Paris

Ettore Arco Isidoro Bugatti was born with all the talent to become a genius: his father Carlo was an important furniture manufacturer, brother Rembrandt a sculptor. Their talents were combined in car-crazy, self-confident Ettore. He designed his first four-cylinder car at the age of 17, won a gold medal for an automobile construction at 20 and went on to become an engineer—today we would say designer—at De Dietrich, Deutz (gas motors), Isotta Fraschini and Peugeot. In 1908, the banker de Viscaya provided financial backing for Ettore's works in Molsheim, completed in 1909, and in 1910, the first five cars rolled off the assembly line. Ettore Bugatti achieved overnight fame when his 1.3-litre Type 13 came second at Le Mans while racing against a Fiat with ten times the cubic capacity. All his successes were based on technical finesse: a sixteen-valve, four-cylinder engine was merely the beginning. Bugatti's cars were immediately recognizable by their horseshoe-shaped radiator. Success on the race course, technical precision and perfection down to the smallest visible and invisible detail made Bugattis the most expensive automobiles of their day. He regarded motor blocks as if they were sculptures, aiming to form the block into a whole with all auxiliary aggregates. Today, designers hide engines in housings. Bugatti, on the other hand, created them as a unit. Wheels became trademark features, as in the Type 35, with eight, flat, silver bands meeting at the centre, a motif in sporty mass-produced models for decades to come.

The crowning achievement of Bugatti's passion and ambition was the Bugatti Royale (Type 41). Construction began in 1926, and the first prototype was completed in 1927. The price tag in 1931 for a car that went over 200 kilometres per hour, had a 12,759-cubic centimetre engine and a 4.3-metre wheel base was correspondingly high: the equivalent of 4 Rolls Royces. This Royale model found three buyers, but it became the classic Bugatti design with horseshoe-shaped radiator and trademark, two-tone paint finish. The most absurd feature of the car was that, where other speedy roadsters among the automotive elite bore allegorical motives of speed, elegance and power, the Royale proudly boasted an elephant rearing up on its hind legs. After the war, the "Magician from Molsheim," the owner of more than a thousand patents, never again produced anything comparable. His brother Roland tried his hand in 1951 with the clumsily drafted Type 101. An attempt to relaunch the name Bugatti in Italy in 1991 produced a 550-horsepower sports car, the EB 110, a car with no design allure. This can be anticipated, however, after two Giugiaro attempts in the most recent Bugatti model, the EB 18/4 Veyron from 1999. It was drafted by Hartmut Warkuss, the top designer at Volkswagen. Porsche descendant and Volkswagen president Piëch insisted on an eighteen-cylinder engine. In true Bugatti fashion, the legend lives on. H.-U. v. M.

This black-blue Royale coupé's wheel base is so wide that a VW Golf could fit between it!

In this model, the mud guards form an elongated S-shape, while the "proud owner" emphasizes the distorted proportions of the car.

(right, bottom)
The Veyron (1999):
the quintessential look
of Bugatti today.

Functional beauty of its time with little space for passengers. Only the silhouette of the bonnet proclaims: "I'm a Bugatti!"

The Type 35, with its ostentatious tyre, sports the most beautiful rims of 1930s racing cars.

Mies van der Rohe's tubular-steel cantilever chair—known as the "MR" chair—was designed in 1927. Since its inception it has been one of the most esteemed icons of the modern movement in architecture and design. Its continued success is largely due to its relaunch by the American furniture company, Knoll Associates, in the 1940s, when it became established as the most desirable chair to offset the purism and high status of modern interiors. It still retains that reputation today.

Mies was not the first architect to exploit the structural properties of tubular steel in chair design. His chair came fast on the heels of earlier cantilevered chair experiments by Dutch architect and designer Mart Stam (1899–1986) and the Bauhaus-educated architect and furniture designer Marcel Breuer (see p. 39). What Mies added to these early initiatives, however, was an aesthetic dimension. Taking Stam's idea he replaced the sharp radii of the curves in the steel tube with a single soft curve which became the hallmark of his design. Mies himself claimed that he was "the first to have consistently exploited the spring quality of steel tubes," as the graceful curve which characterizes the base structure of his chair allows for a high level of flexibility and movement. While Stam and Breuer sought primarily technical solutions (Breuer was inspired by the steel tube used on his bicycle), Mies exploited this new material to create a lasting image of modernity which is visually refined, elegant and harmonious.

The MR chair was not the work of Mies alone. It evolved—as did all his furniture pieces designed in the short period between 1927 and 1930—from a collaboration with the designer Lilly Reich (1885–1947). Together they made the sketches become a reality. Reich was responsible, for example, for the wickerwork used for the seat and back in one of the models. The alternative material used for this purpose was belting fabric. Both models appeared at the Weissenhof housing complex project at "The Dwelling" exhibition organized by the Deutscher Werkbund and held in Stuttgart in 1927. Their impact was significant. However, it took a few years to get the design manufactured efficiently. The first models, made by the Joseph Müller Metal Company and subsequently by the Bamberg Metal Workshops, were essentially handmade chairs which were inevitably expensive to purchase. By 1932, the Thonet company had taken over manufacture of the MR chair, and a new level of rationalization entered into its production.

In terms of Mies's oeuvre, the chair stands alongside the "Barcelona" chair which was produced a couple of years later. From the beginning of his career as an architect, Mies had designed furniture pieces for his buildings, using wood in the early days. Tubular steel offered him the possibility of finding a furniture language which suited the pure minimalism of his buildings and which helped articulate the spatial poetry of his architectural designs. The elegance of the MR chair, combined with its compatibility with the language of modern architecture, has made it one of the most significant furniture designs of the twentieth century.

P.S.

Ludwig Mies van der Rohe

1886   Born on March 27 in Aachen, Germany
1899–03 Draftsman for stucco decoration and ornament in Aachen workshops
1905–07 Apprenticeship under Bruno Paul; also studies at the School for Arts and Crafts, Munich
1908–11 Works for Peter Behrens, Berlin
1911   Begins as self-employed architect, Berlin
1925–26 Furniture group in laminated wood for his own Berlin apartment
1927   German patent for *Stahlrohrfreischwinger* (tubular-steel cantilever chair), manufactured by the Joseph Müller Metal Company ("MR" series); Head of the Deutscher Werkbund exhibition "The Dwelling" in Stuttgart (Weissenhof housing complex); collaboration with Lilly Reich
1929   German Pavilion at the "International Exhibition" in Barcelona ("Barcelona" chair)
1928   Tugendhat House in Brünn (now Brno, Czech Republic); interior design in the following years
1929–30 "Tugendhat" chair; "Brno" chair; couch (also used in Farnsworth House)
1930–33 Last director of the Bauhaus in Dessau and Berlin
1931   The Bamberg Metal Workshops, Berlin, takes over his furniture line; in November 1931, he signs a contract with Thonet, which produces the MR chair as of 1932; Head of the department "Die Wohnung unserer Zeit" at the Bauausstellung, Berlin
1938   Emigrates to the United States; opens architectural practice in Chicago
1948   Licensed production of furniture facsimiles by Knoll Associates, New York, in slightly changed form
1951–58 Lake Shore Drive apartments, Chicago
1954–58 Seagram Building, New York (with Philip Johnson)
1969   Dies on August 17 in Chicago

A modern classic: the tubular-steel cantilever chair, 1927.

Illustration from *Der Stuhl* (The Chair), a publication by Heinz Bodo Rasch, 1928.

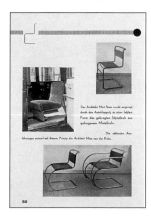

SIDE TABLE E-1027

Eileen Gray

Eileen Gray

1878	Born on August 9 in Enniscorthy, Ireland
1898–02	Studies painting and drawing at the Slade School of Fine Art, London; learns lacquerwork techniques (from 1900 onwards) in D. Charles's furniture workshop
1902–05	Studies in Paris successively at the Ecole Colarossi and the Académie Julian
1907	Works with the Japanese lacquerwork specialist, Seizo Sugawara, in Paris
1914	Designs a number of pieces of lacquerwork furniture for Jacques Doucet's house in Paris
1919–22	Furnishings for an apartment for Suzanne Talbot in Paris
1922–30	Maintains a gallery in Paris under the name Jean Désert, where she sells her work
1923	Displays a controversial interior "Boudoir for Monte Carlo" at the Salon of the Société des Artistes Décorateurs
1927–29	Builds own E-1027 house in Roquebrune (in cooperation with Jean Badovici); designs pieces for the interior, including the "Transat" deckchair and the E-1027 side table
1929	"Bibendum" easy chair
1930–31	Apartment for Jean Badovici, Paris
1932–34	Private house "Tempe à Pailla," Castellar; designs the furnishings, including the "S" chair
1976	Dies on November 28 in Paris

The Irish designer Eileen Gray, originally a painter, spent the first third of her career in her Paris atelier crafting lacquer finishes and furniture oriented towards the Japanese tradition. Until 1930, she distributed her work primarily to well-to-do private clients from the world of fashion and society through her own small business. Not until the age of 49, encouraged through her acquaintance with Le Corbusier as much as by the admiration of the Dutch De Stijl group (which had helped her in 1924 on a special issue of the magazine *Wendingen*), she built her first house as an autodidact.

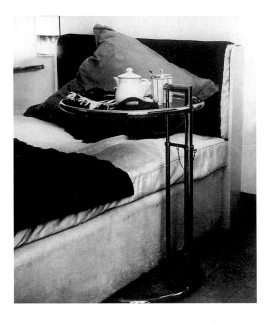

The table's adjustable height was originally designed for breakfast in bed, 1927.

Multifunctional and diverse, this tubular-steel design has a timeless appeal.

Located in Roquebrune at Cap Martin on the French Riviera, the house has come to be regarded as a paradigm of the architectural "Moderne." The adjustable small side table was designed for this house and became known, like the house itself, by the designation "E-1027." Seen in a somewhat romantic reading, the *E* stands for "Eileen" and the numbers, corresponding to their sequence in the alphabet, stand for *J*, *B* and *G*. The second and tenth letter would be an allusion to her friend and mentor, the Rumanian architect Jean Badovici (1892–1956). Gray had already experimented with steel pipe previous to 1927, thereby anticipating certain designs of her famous colleagues such as Ludwig Mies van der Rohe (see p. 45), Marcel Breuer (see p. 39), Charlotte Perriand (b. 1903) and Le Corbusier (see p. 48).

The side table is probably her most famous creation and has been plagiarized countless times to our day. It was part of a revolutionary series of furniture pieces, all designed for this house. This included the technical "Transat" deckchair, the "Bibendum" chair (made of horizontally stacked leather rolls) and the asymmetrical armchair "Nonconformist." These furniture pieces are distinguished by variability, flexibility, esprit and elegance, while having that human dimension which prevents them from falling into the rigidity of formulas and programmatic statements found in other steel pipe furniture of her male colleagues. With Gray, the functionalist imperative is always humanized through grace. Variability, folding- and sliding-systems are the predominant characteristics. This can be seen in the table which, because of its concentric asymmetry, can be slid under a bed, raised by lockable telescope legs or carried about by virtue of its light weight. The three-quarter-circle feet, like the table ring and the double-pipe leg, is made of stainless steel pipe, while the table leaf is nearly always made of glass. A handle at the end of the double pipe increases both function and comfort. Originally created as a prototype and praised by Le Corbusier, like the entire house, as "enchanting and refined," the E-1027 side table has become one of the most desired furnishings of the twentieth century. Today, the re-edition rights are in the sole possession of the ClassiCon Company in Munich. V.F.

Contemporary re-edition from ClassiCon, Munich.

CHAISE LONGUE LC4

Le Corbusier

Le Corbusier

1887   Born Charles-Edouard Jeanneret on October 6 in La Chaux-de-Fonds, Switzerland

1900–04 Trains as an engraver under Charles L'Eplattenier in La Chaux-de-Fonds

1907   Villa Fallet, La Chaux-de-Fonds

1908   Works in the atelier of Auguste Perret, Paris

1910–11 Works for Peter Behrens, Berlin

1912–16 Head of an atelier for Arts and Crafts in La Chaux-de-Fonds

1916   Villa Schwob, La Chaux-de-Fonds

1917   Moves to Paris; publication of *Après le cubisme* with Amedée Ozenfant

1920–25 Co-publisher of the magazine *L'Esprit Nouveau*

1922   Begins collaboration with his cousin Pierre Jeanneret

1923–25 Publication of *Vers une architecture* under the pseudonym "Le Corbusier"; La Roche-Jeanneret duplex house, Paris

1925   Pavillon de l'Esprit Nouveau at the Exposition des Arts Décoratifs, Paris

1927   Two apartment buildings at the Weissenhof housing complex, Stuttgart

1928   Co-founder of the Congrès Internationaux d'Architecture Moderne (CIAM)

1929–31 Villa Savoye; furniture designs for the Paris Fall Salon with Charlotte Perriand

1930   Becomes a French citizen

1947–52 First realization of a "Unité d'habitation" in Marseille

1950   Develops the "Modulor" as a proportional scale for housing design and furnishings

1950–55 Chapel of Notre-Dame-du-Haut, Ronchamp

1952–65 Buildings in Ahmedabad and planning of the city of Chandigarh, India

1957–60 Monastery Sainte-Marie-de-La-Tourette, Eveux

1965   Dies on August 27 in Roquebrune at Cap Martin, France

Many of the chairs designed by the architect Le Corbusier are now design classics of the twentieth century. Among these is the "Chaise Longue LC4" of 1928, one of the most stylish and elegant of its type. The ponyskin cover of the seat is stretched on a tubular-steel frame. This in turn rests on an H-shaped steel tube base. Manufactured originally by Thonet, the chair was reissued in 1965 by the Italian manufacturer Cassina. With its movable seat section and adjustable head rest, it is an early example of ergonomic design. Its use of ponyskin for its seat cover followed a contemporary fashion for animal skins in upholstery.

This chaise longue was originally one of three types of chairs designed by Le Corbusier between 1928 and 1929. Each combined the use of tubular-steel frames with leather or skin upholstery. The other two, the "Grand Confort" chair of 1928 and the "Basculant" chair of 1929 were also initially manufactured by Thonet. All three were used by Le Corbusier as part of the furniture for private French house commissions including the Villa Savoye, Poissy (1929–31) and the Villa d'Avray. The clean, sleek lines of the chaise longue and his other chairs complemented the interiors of his private villas with their elevated concrete construction, open-plan spaces, ribbon windows and cantilevered façades resting on column supports.

Le Corbusier's building for the Pavillon de l'Esprit Nouveau, at the 1925 Paris Exposition des Arts Décoratifs, exemplified this purist aesthetic, featuring plain walls without mouldings, plate-glass windows, modular building components, standardized unit furniture and abstract paintings by Fernand Léger (1881–1955). At the Paris Salon d'Automne of 1929, Le Corbusier, Pierre Jeanneret (1896–1967) and Charlotte Perriand (b. 1903) carried these ideas a step further, exhibiting a modern apartment with concealed lighting and laminated surfaces, furnished with free-standing chairs and table and a built-in storage wall with shelving, storage drawers, glass-fronted display boxes and mirrored, sliding-door cabinets. While Le Corbusier's furniture designs form a small part of his total volume of work as an architect, nonetheless they have had a lasting impact. Their stylish elegance, together with the subtleness of their designs, has ensured their enduring appeal.   D.B.

Le Corbusier's design sketches, ca. 1928.

The LC4 is available in three covers:
black leather, patterned pony or
calf hide and natural, tear-resistant
canvas—today manufactured by
Cassina.

The LC4 installed at the
La Roche-Jeanneret duplex houses,
built by Le Corbusier (1923–25),
and today home of the Le Corbusier
Foundation, Paris.

LONDON UNDERGROUND MAP

Edward Johnston

The first line in the London Underground system was the Metropolitan Line, opened in 1863 and running between Paddington and Farringdon. Over the next 70 years, the vigour and competitive stamina of classic capitalistic entrepreneurship created for London an almost inextricable web of 165 independent companies running a public transport system of buses and underground trains. Each company displayed its identity in the uniforms worn by its staff, the rolling stock and its stations, which were sometimes situated no more than 100 yards away from a competitor. In 1924, an advisory committee advised the Minster of Transport to do something about "the acute and wasteful competition," but it took until 1931 to set up London Transport. To Frank Pick, the first managing director, it was clear that the new company would stand no chance of success unless its employees were able to identify it as an efficient unit. His decision to use design for this purpose was something quite new for the time. His approach to design was largely based on the ideals of John Ruskin and William Morris, who, in the nineteenth century, saw design as a means of enlightenment, a way of raising the intellectual level of the public. But Pick did something else with design, something quite new for his day, by introducing it as a way of uniting a group of companies, each with its own style, under a single new visual identity. What the public saw was a consistent service, combined with a bright, recognizable design for the stations so that travellers would perceive the new company as a single unit. Essentially, Pick introduced a single, consistent visual framework and in so doing created the first fully integrated "corporate identity." Architects were invited to build new stations and graphic designers to design posters, the lettering to be used for station names and the route maps. Edward Johnston designed a new typeface and logo for the names of the stations. The buses, which were painted red, had a logo designed specially for them.

On his own initiative, Harry Beck, one of the company's electricians, designed a map based on an electronic circuit diagram. After a few rejections he was given the chance to work out his idea in more detail. The straight lines, uniform terminations and 45-degree angles provided a representation of London that was abstract rather than geographical. The scale was not fixed, so that the map was able to reach from the centre all the way to the outer suburbs. In fact, the map was much more than a schematic representation of the London Underground. The recognizable shape and well-known names such as Victoria Station, Oxford Circus, Piccadilly Circus and Leicester Square made this map much more than a diagram of a transport system: it was London as people imagined it. R.K.

Edward Johnston

1872	Born on February 11 in Uruguay Studies medicine; parallel calligraphy studies at the School of the British Museum, London, with W. R. Lathaby
1898–01	Teaches calligraphy at the London Council's Central School of Arts and Crafts
1902	Begins teaching at the Royal Academy, London
1903–05	Illuminated capitals for the Doves Bible
1906	Publishes the book *Writing and Illuminating and Lettering* in London
1907	Marries the calligrapher Florence Kingsford
1909	Typography for the Doves Press edition of Shakespeare's *Hamlet*
1913–14	Works for the trade magazine *The Imprint*
1929	Typography for the Cranach Press edition of *Hamlet*, Weimar
1944	Dies on November 26 in Witchling, Sussex

(right)
The Underground map, structured like an electronic switching circuit, greatly facilitates readability and orientation in comparison to the original geographic representation.

With this geometric, Sans Serif typeface, Johnston created a corporate identity for the London Underground system.

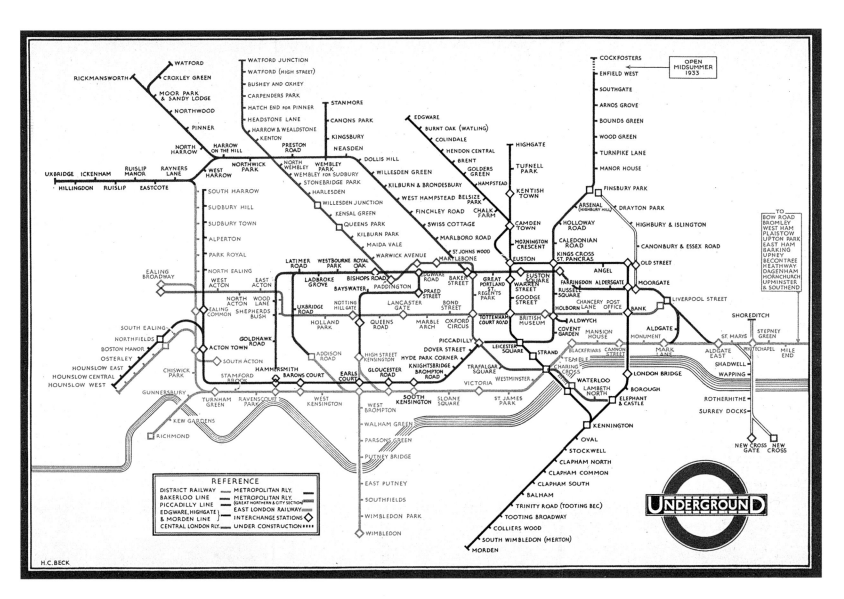

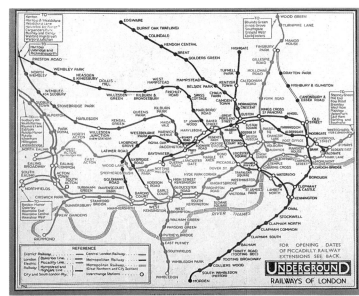

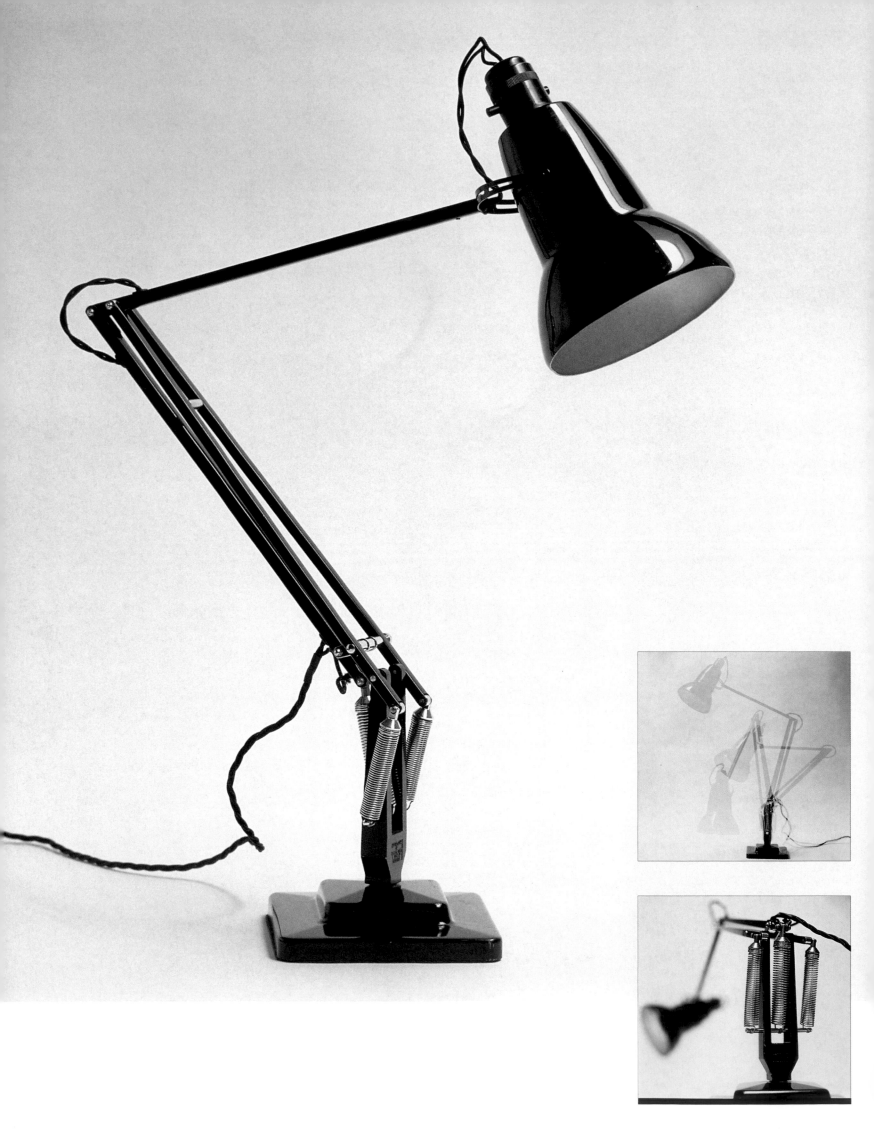

ANGLEPOISE LAMP

George Carwardine

Minimal, functional design:
the Anglepoise lamp is one
of the most successful lamps
of the twentieth century.

Ever since its invention, the Anglepoise lamp has remained a firm favourite for adjustable lighting in the home and office. It was developed in 1932 by an English engineer, George Carwardine (1887–1948). The Anglepoise retains its popularity today for its combination of sturdiness and flexibility of light positions. The basic concept rests on the design of its arm support. This incorporates a series of carefully counterbalanced springs which maintain the tension of the lamp's arm, enabling it to be adjusted into position, and then to hold that posture, thus mimicking the function of the human arm.

Carwardine started his career in the automobile industry. From an initial engineering apprenticeship in his native city of Bath in 1912, he joined the Horstmann Car Company, becoming both its works manager and chief designer in 1916. During the 1920s he ran his own business, Carwardine Associates, designing and manufacturing automobile suspension systems, among other components. It was during this phase that Carwardine's interest in the basic principles of the Anglepoise lamp began. His fascination with springs, weights and sliding mechanisms prompted him to experiment with an apparatus which could move through three planes but then hold in any position. The springs for Carwardine's prototype lamps proved difficult to manufacture, because they had to be twisted so tightly. This prompted him to collaborate with a prominent British firm of spring manufacturers, Herbert Terry of Redditch. Together they perfected the new lamp, patenting it in 1932, and manufacturing commenced in 1933.

The lamp was initially designed for industrial applications, but it soon became popular for use in the home and office. Terry's entered into an agreement with Carwardine, who developed variants on the Anglepoise for a variety of different settings, including hospital wards, operating theatres and the Royal Mail.

During the Second World War, Carwardine worked on projects for the Ministry of Defence, including rotors and developments in tank suspension. He also devised a miniature Anglepoise lamp, made specifically for the navigators' cockpits in Wellington bomber aircraft. An example of this is now in the collection of the Design Museum, London. Anglepoise lamps have also been featured in films and on television: in the James Bond films, they are used by "Q" section's scientists. In *Indiana Jones and The Last Crusade* (1989), Sean Connery and Harrison Ford use an Anglepoise lamp while deciphering codes.

An appealing factor of the
Anglepoise lamp is its stability,
regardless of any position.

In 1971, Anglepoise was bought by the world's largest spring manufacturer, the Associated Spring Corporation of the United States. In 1975, the managing director of Anglepoise, John Terry, grandson of the original manufacturer, formed a partnership with his cousin Ray to buy back the company, returning it to private ownership. Today, the company continues to flourish in Redditch, England, manufacturing a range of task lighting and accessories, including the ever-popular Anglepoise lamp. Although its design has evolved over the years, its basic principles remain intact. A true design classic, it was recently voted favourite lamp in a poll of 50 of Europe's design *cognoscenti*.   D.B.

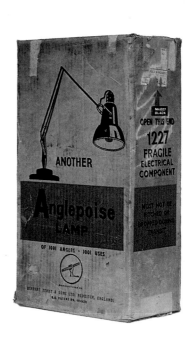

BIALETTI MOKA EXPRESS

Alfonso Bialetti

A functional diagram of the Moka Express.

One of the most stylish coffee makers produced for domestic use is the Moka Express, first designed and developed in Italy in 1933 by Alfonso Bialetti. Its faceted and waisted shape gives it a distinctive appearance. The cast-aluminium body and Bakelite knob and handle convey effective heat transmission and protection, respectively. Its design excellence has been recognized by the Museum of Modern Art, New York, which owns an example. Bialetti, its manufacturers, claim that it is the only industrial object which has remained unchanged since its inception.

In 1918, Bialetti, who had trained as a metalworker, opened a small metalworking shop in Crusinallo, in the Italian province of Novarra. From making small metal products for the home, Bialetti had graduated to experiments with coffee pot design—he had learnt aluminium casting techniques in Paris, where he had spent six years. From his early experiments, Bialetti developed the distinctive form of the Moka Express.

The Moka Express coffee maker consists of three metal parts: the base boiler compartment, which is gravity cast; a filter section for the ground coffee, through which the boiling water is forced under pressure; and an upper compartment with an integral spout, which is pressure-cast and from which the brewed coffee is then poured. Aluminium is used for the manufacture of the body, because of its effectiveness in retaining and transmitting heat and because of its porosity, which allows it to absorb the flavour of the coffee. In fact, the flavour of the liquid brew becomes more aromatic and intense with each boiling. The knob of the lid and the handle are made out of Bakelite, which is highly heat-resistant, and the internal compartment for the ground coffee is still fabricated manually.

Between 1934 and 1939, Bialetti made 70,000 examples. Production ceased during the Second World War. When peace returned, Bialetti was joined by his son Renato, who proved to have a gift for business. During the 1950s, Bialetti mounted a highly effective marketing and advertising campaign. The strategy proved successful. A new factory was constructed and completed in 1956. Here, 4 million coffee makers are produced annually. In 1993, Bialetti was acquired by the Rondini group, which has retained the coffee maker's original name. Such is their popularity that Bialetti coffee makers have been widely copied, but these copies cannot compete with the originals which use aluminium that has been smelted once only. Worldwide, over 200 million Moka Express coffee makers have been sold since 1933, representing 65 per cent of the world market. This is topped by Swedes and Finns consuming on average 9 cups of coffee daily; Italians consume 4 cups, with 90 per cent of Italian households owning a Bialetti Moka Express.   D.B.

This clever advertising campaign for the Moka Express was a boost for Bialetti's sales.

A symbol of Italian lifestyle, the Moka Express is exported worldwide as a simple and inexpensive product.

VOLKSEMPFÄNGER (PEOPLE'S RADIO)

Walter Maria Kersting

Walter Maria Kersting

1889	Born on July 8 in Münster, Germany
ca. 1910	Works in his father's architecture office
1912–14	Studies engineering and architecture at the Technical School, Hannover
1918–22	Employed as a graphic designer
1923–27	Artistic director at Krauss-Werke, Schwarzenberg
1926	Appointed professor at the School for Applied Art, Cologne
1932	Publishes the book *Lebendige Form*
1928–33	Designs the "VE 301" *Volksempfänger*
1933–44	Teaches graphic design at the State Academy of Fine Arts, Düsseldorf
1945	Carries on his work in his studio in Waging, Germany
1952–58	Designs various telephone sets for Telephonbau und Normalzeit, Frankfurt
1953	Co-founder of the Rat für Formgebung (Committee for Form)
1954	Opens office in Düsseldorf
1962	Designs machine tools for Pfauter, Ludwigsburg
1970	Dies on May 5 in Waging, Germany

The ideals of twentieth-century modernism were manifested differently in the United States versus Europe and expressed either a collectively optimistic future or anticipated a horrifying end. Despite these differences, what they had in common was their fascination for industrial technology and mass production. The machine, in particular, was seen as the ultimate metaphor for the modernists' concepts of speed and mobility, repetition and rhythm—the mass as opposed to the individual. The aircraft, the car, the telephone and also the radio were the new technological inventions of the modern era and thus were also the visual and ideological symbols of modernism. The first radios appeared on the market around 1925 and were originally seen as toys for electronic hobbyists. It took only a few years for the radio to develop into a product with universal appeal and for its significance as a method of communication to be appreciated.

Walter Maria Kersting's design for a mass-produced *Volksempfänger* (People's Radio) was a bizarre paradox. Produced in Bakelite, an outstanding example of an industrial material, it contained all the essential design elements made famous by the Bauhaus and was in keeping with the ideology practised there. The aim of the Bauhaus was to design new kinds of industrial products, using high-tech materials, which could be mass-produced. The idea for the *Volksempfänger* also came from the same powers that in 1932 closed down the Bauhaus as "un-German." The design—one might say the Bauhaus design—however, acquired a totally different emotional content; one that embodied the triumph of German technological

The totalitarian regime of the Third Reich exploited the new technology as a tool for propaganda.

The *Volksempfänger*'s simple, geometric shape and Bakelite material made mass production and a low price feasible.

Walter Dorwin Teague
Biography, see p. 64

ingenuity and industrial strength—two crucial elements in the supremacy of a darker ideological power. Even its function was pressed into the service of this power, which used it as the first industrial tool to manipulate the thoughts and desires of a whole nation. This radio, which was only capable of receiving broadcasts from German transmitters, acted as the mouthpiece of those in power to explain, manipulate and legitimize collective consciousness and behaviour and took only a few years to contribute to the undermining of the German critical and intellectual tradition.

By contrast, and designed after the *Volksempfänger*, Walter Dorwin Teague's Blue Moon radio reflected the romantic American dream both literally and metaphorically. This dream promised comfort, happiness and unlimited welfare for everyone who "bought American," thus helping to pull the country out of the deep economic and social crisis of the 1930s. Consumption was praised as an act of patriotism. The Hollywood films of the 1930s, designed to make the glorious future visible at the time, were also mass-produced messengers of collective happiness. The designers of the day—Norman Bel Geddes, Henry Dreyfuss, Raymond Loewy, Harold van Doren, Walter Dorwin Teague, Donald Deskey—were treated like film stars. The apotheosis to this "highway to the future" was the 1939 New York World's Fair, celebrating "The Dawn of Tomorrow" while the Second World War, which broke out shortly thereafter, became the testing ground. R. K.

The American dream: in the 1930s, a Blue Moon radio was a *must* for any U.S. household.

ZIPPO LIGHTER

George Blaisdell

George Blaisdell with his Zippo lighter.

One of the first models, 1933.

Invented in 1933 by Californian George Blaisdell (1895–1978), the Zippo "windproof" lighter has become an archetypal American design icon on a par with the distinctive styling of Coca-Cola bottles (see p. 28), Harley Davidson motorcycles (see p. 136) and Levi's jeans. Originally retailing at $1.95, this chrome-plated lighter was designed to fit neatly into the palm of the hand and had a hinged lid which enabled the user to open and use it with only one hand. Fabricated from rectangular brass tubing with the hinge soldered to the outside, it also incorporated a windshield around the flame as a means of making it easy to use in adverse conditions. Although the hinge was removed from the outside of the case in 1936, there have been comparatively few substantive changes to the design since it was first introduced. Well over 300 million have been sold. Fundamental to its phenomenal success was Blaisdell's brilliant marketing tactic—the offering of a lifetime warranty and free repair for any defects, a policy which still holds today.

The Zippo's integration into the American way of life was ensured by its use by American troops in the Second World War. Between 1943 and 1945, the U.S. government ordered the entire production of Zippo lighters for distribution to Army and Navy personnel, ensuring an important place in countless stories of wartime exploits. Military associations continued in subsequent wars with American involvement in Korea, Vietnam and the Persian Gulf. Indeed, countless tales have been told of the Zippo's use as a signalling device in rescue operations, its ability to deflect bullets when carried in the breast pocket of military fatigues or even its capacity for heating soup in upturned helmets. It also has been featured in numerous wartime movies and film noir classics, marked by the introduction of dramatic pauses in the action whilst the ritual of lighting a cigarette, accompanied by the distinctive click of the Zippo lighter and a deep intake of breath, is enacted. Over the decades it has continued to be profiled, as in more recent films such as *Indiana Jones and the Last Crusade* (1989) and *Terminator 2* (1991) with actors including Bruce Willis, Harrison Ford, Arnold Schwarzenegger and Sean Connery making use of it in a variety of ways.

The Zippo's role as an American icon is further underlined by its frequent associations with American history, whether in terms of the commemorative issues concerned with NASA space exploration, the 1976 bicentennial celebrations, the National Football League, the Wild West, the Civil War or famous presidents. However, by the mid-1980s, the company found it necessary to adopt a more aggressive approach for American consumers, specifically targeting the gift, souvenir and collector market. The last became especially important and remunerative with the growing strength of the anti-smoking lobby in the United States. Steps were also taken to widen the company's product range into flashlights, pens, belt buckles and other products geared to the 18 to 34 age group. Franchises for the name were exercised in important foreign markets such as Japan (the company's leading market outside the United States) and linked to such archetypal American products as jeans. In 1997, the Zippo Company bought W. R. Case & Sons Cutlery, a well-known manufacturer of knives sought after by collectors, and opened a 15,000-square-foot Zippo-Case Visitors Center in Bradford, Pennsylvania, complete with museum, interactive displays and retail outlet.   J. M.W.

Film still from *Black Rain* (1989) with Andy Garcia and Michael Douglas.

The Zippo's protective windshield, attached to the case, made it a big success.

PENCIL SHARPENER

Raymond Loewy

Raymond Loewy

The American industrial designers of the 1930s saw streamlined design as a visual symbol impinging on everyday life. As they saw it, this kind of design went with the new industrial civilization which was to bring mankind unlimited prosperity and happiness. They saw themselves as the creators of an individual, aesthetic manifestation of this ideal. In the 1930s the United States experienced an almost revolutionary transformation from what was socio-economically still a predominantly rural society—with traditional values such as thrift and an unshakable faith in religion, order and authority—into a centralized urban society with weaker social ties and a competitively egocentric economy directed towards mass consumption.

The designer saw his task as being to clean up the past. He deformed old-fashioned machines and pieces of equipment by softening their lines and covering them up, turning them into mysterious mechanisms, with no apparent need for oil or grease, whose works were no longer visible. Every civilized item was covered up. The open, angular cars of the "Roaring Twenties" became closed and rounded, and the transparent, cheerful, austere Dixieland jazz was transformed into the flexible, concealed modulations of Swing. Film became a glamorous pink country for a middle class craving romance and happy endings. In the comic strips, Flash Gordon and Buck Rogers raced through the galaxy in streamlined spaceships surrounded by long-legged, scantily dressed, full-busted young women.

The streamlined style was indissolubly linked with the socioeconomic mechanisms of mass production and mass consumption of the years 1934–55, when new models were introduced yearly so as to encourage the consumer to exchange the old for the new—guaranteeing greater happiness. Understandably, this came to be seen as the art form of industrial capitalism.

The characteristics of streamlined design were shiny, severely rounded and enclosed shapes with horizontal lines to reinforce the suggestion of movement. There was an obsession with the visual symbolism of hygiene and health, with direct Freudian references to masculinity and sexuality. Designs referred to movement as a metaphor for progress, Darwinian evolution and constant change.

The teardrop form—a drop of water viewed at the moment immediately before its fall—was seen as the ideal streamlined shape. It was seen as the ideal body, the shape with the least possible air resistance. The drop took on almost mythical qualities in the eyes of designers and constantly recurred in sketches of cars, city buses, ships, aircraft and everyday products for the home and office such as thermos flasks, pencil boxes, irons, radios and items of furniture. Raymond Loewy's pencil sharpener is the clearest possible example. Though only a prototype exists (it never went into production), it is the perfect blueprint of the mythical obsession with anything streamlined. Further, it is a high-class paradox in which a trivial appliance, which should really be an inconspicuous item standing ready for use at the corner of the desk, is transformed into a futuristic sculpture seemingly capable of blasting off into outer space.   R.K.

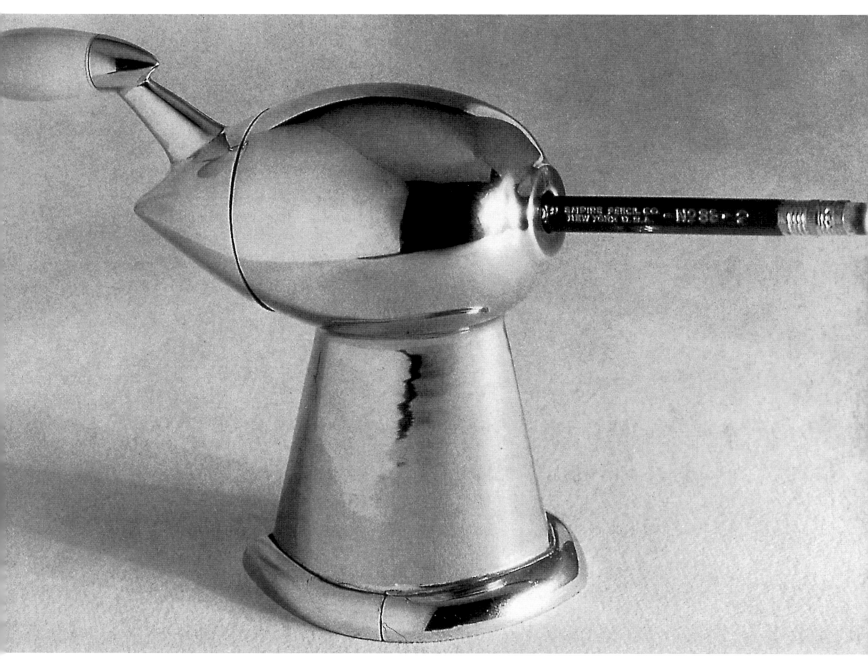

In the streamline style: Loewy's
prototype for a teardrop-shaped pencil
sharpener was never mass produced.

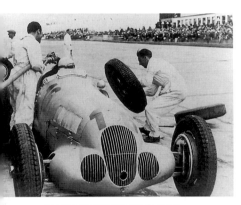

The 750-kilogram Formula featured a three-part "face," mid-1930s.

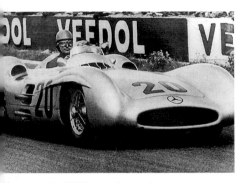

The W 196 streamlined version had a hood flatter than its wings and a perfect oval for ventilation, 1954.

The W 196 Monoposto featured a wide-opened mouth, 1954.

Legends are often born by chance. Daimler importer Jellinek's daughter was named Mercedes, and, in 1901, it became the name of a new car model that he was promoting. The new Mercedes racing car was called "Silver Arrow" because a new 750-kilogram Formula in 1934 inspired racing director Alfred Neubauer to scrape 2 kilograms of white paint from the aluminium skin of the "fireballs" in order to reduce their weight. Ever since, Silver Arrow has been the generic name for a racing car from Stuttgart too powerful for any ordinary road.

World champion several times over before the Second World War (against tough competition from Italy), the Mercedes was able to defend its title in the face of all new Formula changes. Their racing cars subscribed to a classic concept with a front-end engine and open wheel wells—the moulding was only gradually extended to cover the wheel suspensions—and it took until the early 1950s before Silver Arrows were acknowledged as a distinct category.

After the initial (post-war) ban on racing, Mercedes approached the track with the "SL" sports version, whose engineering was based on the 300 series (also called the "Adenauer" because it was the chancellor's official car). It was built for long-distance races such as the Mille Miglia in Italy or the 1952 Carrera Panamericana in Mexico. In body type, it resembled the hard-top coupés. Instead of an integral frame, the aluminium skin was stretched across a filigree tubular frame from which it deflected in the lower end to allow for the door cut-outs. Extending the door into the roof, where it was hinge-fastened, compensated for the lack of door height. This design created the unforgettable and often-copied wing doors so characteristic of this model.

For its Formula 1 entry in 1954, Mercedes used a unique approach in the W 196. Fast tracks were driven with the streamlined version, winding courses with the open wheel-well design; the driver's seat was centrally positioned in both, and yet both were to define the style of all subsequent Mercedes sports-car models. The open wheel-well model had to assert itself with a broad yet elegant front grille against narrow-fronted competitors. The solidly moulded streamlined version used its one-piece skin to stylistic advantage, be it with the "fins" above the wheel cut-outs, the lateral ventilation grilles or the ventilation slit beneath the windscreen.

Outside pressure, this time from U.S. general manager Maxie Hoffmann, prompted Mercedes, in 1954, to build the "tame" SL version for daily use with the formal details of the W 196 streamlined model: fins, gills and flat bonnet, thanks to a strongly tilted engine. An "economy model," the 190 SL, rolled off the assembly line at the same time. But only the sports and racing models were true Silver Arrows, and the old 300 SL and the SLR to be launched for sale in 2002 still bask in their glamour. H.-U.v. M.

The 300 SL made history with its unique wing-doors, 1954.

The 300 SL Roadster introduced vertical headlights and eliminated the wing-doors, 1958.

Study for the SLR, which joined Formula I looks with Silver Arrow genes and included many new features, 1999.

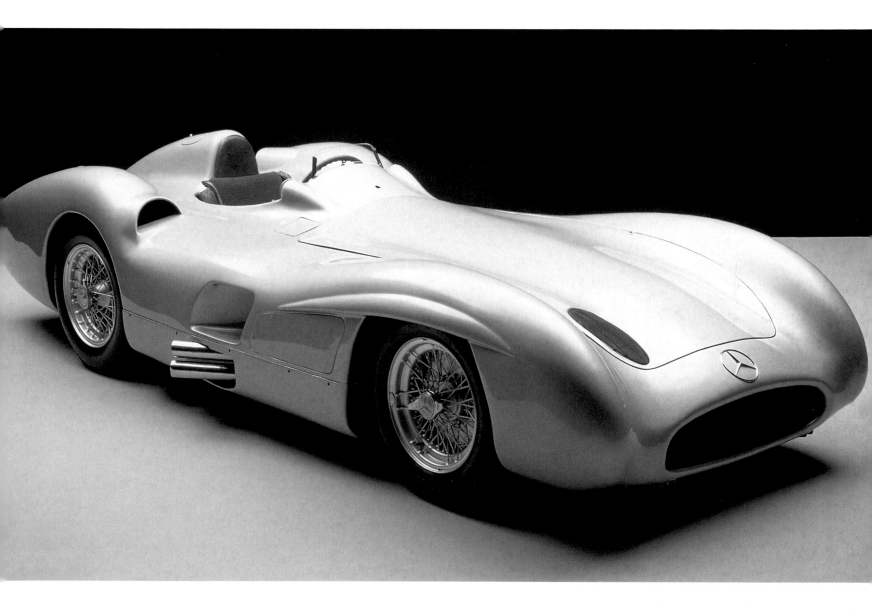

The 300 SLR came out
decades before the new
Smart car's motto
"Reduce to the Max"
or "Less is More," 1955.

The 300 SLR featured a
knock-out brake block, 1955.

KODAK BABY BROWNIE CAMERA

Walter Dorwin Teague

Walter Dorwin Teague

1883   Born on December 18 in Decatur, Indiana

1903–07   Attends evening classes at the New York Art Students League

1908–10   Works as a graphic designer with the Calkins & Holdin advertising agency, New York

1911–26   Active as freelance graphic designer in his own office in New York

1926   After his return from a trip through Europe, where he studied the work of Le Corbusier, concentrates on industrial design

1928–60   Works for Eastman Kodak, Rochester, New York; designs such models as the "Baby Brownie" (1934) and the "Bantam Special" (1936)

1930   Marmon Model 16 car (in cooperation with Walter Dorwin Teague Jnr.)

1933–34   Ford Pavilion at Chicago's Century of Progress Exposition

1934–36   Various radio receivers for Sparton Corporation, Jackson, Michigan, including the model "1186 Nocturne"

1935–37   House style for Texaco petrol stations

1939   Member of the Board of Design for the New York World's Fair; designs pavilions for this exhibition for companies such as Du Pont, Ford and National Cash Register

1940   Publishes the book *Design This Day: The Technique of Order in the Machine Age*; co-founder and first chairman of the American Society of Industrial Designers

1956   Interior of the 707 Boeing aircraft, Seattle, Washington

1960   Dies on December 5 in Flemington, New Jersey

American designer Walter Dorwin Teague worked as a design consultant for the Kodak Company from 1928. With a background in graphic design and illustration, he shifted his focus to industrial design after a European journey in 1926. Within a few years, he became one of America's most recognized and respected figures in this new branch of professional design; he worked, among others, for the Ford Motor company (salesrooms, exhibition architecture) and for the airplane industry (Boeing—the Boeing works in Seattle are still linked with Teague's studio today). In his book *Design This Day: The Technique of Order in the Machine Age* (1940), Teague proved himself to be a thoughtful and discerning observer and co-creator of North America's visual universe.

Teague was the designer of the 1934 Kodak Baby Brownie camera, which did much to popularize photography. The Kodak marketing team aimed for a retail price of just one dollar so as to match the price of the first Kodak "Brownie" in 1900. The intention was to greatly increase the consumption of film (film-roll format) with the attractive-looking Baby Brownie in order to create a new mass market. The camera therefore had to be as simple as possible in construction and operation. The Baby Brownie is a fair-weather camera with a fixed stop and only one shutter speed. The compact body (6 centimetres high, 8 centimetres wide, 7 centimetres deep) was made of plastic: the brown model in Bakelite and the black model in galalith. The vertical grooves on the front panel, continued on the top, looked appealing and conveniently drew attention away from the furrow between the two halves of the body. The construction was ingenious in its simplicity. The body surrounded a mechanism firmly connected to the top; to load a new roll of film, this mechanism could be pulled out like a drawer. The fixed lens, too, was made of plastic. The precision of the duroplast body had to be such that the interior of the housing was completely sealed off against light without additional sealing strips. Its consistency of marketing approach, construction and form make the Baby Brownie exemplary of modern design for a consumer society. It was enormously successful—manufactured and sold by the millions. Most images taken with these cameras probably ended up, unenlarged, as contact prints in family albums.   C.L.

The first Kodak Brownie was introduced in 1900; it featured inexpensive materials and was easy to operate.

In 1934, the Kodak Baby Brownie was sold for just
one dollar so as to increase photography's mass appeal.

HINDENBURG ZEPPELIN

Ferdinand Graf von Zeppelin

The first dirigible, the LZ-I, hovering above Lake Constance, 1900.

Ferdinand Graf von Zeppelin

1838	Born on July 8 in Constance, Germany. Studies mechanical engineering, chemistry and political science at the Polytechnic in Stuttgart, at the War College in Tübingen and at the University of Tübingen
1858	Cavalry officer
1891	Leaves military service; constructs an airship in collaboration with Theodor Kobers
1892–93	Constructs a rigid airship
1898	Founds the Gesellschaft zur Förderung der Luftschiffahrt AG (Society for the Advancement of Airship Travel)
1900	Launches LZ-1 on July 2
1905	Begins collaboration with Hugo Eckener
1908	After the explosion of the LZ-4, a fundraising drive enables continuation at the newly founded Luftschiffahrt Zeppelin GmbH, Friedrichshafen
1909	Construction of a steel hanger for production; later, construction of wind tunnels
1917	Dies on March 8 in Berlin

Graf von Zeppelin's dirigible airships were perceived as aesthetic visual experiences and erotic metaphors, which certainly must have contributed to the zeppelin's enormous popularity. Perhaps Sigmund Freud was correct when he described the first zeppelin as "a powerful dream symbol of the male genital." But the zeppelin also fulfilled the nineteenth-century dream of being able to fly and the long-standing human desire to sail through the ocean of the sky, to float nimbly between the clouds, lighter than air. Flying was also perceived as a way to escape a bourgeois world full of conventions.

In 1895, after dozens of experiments in France and the United States, many of which ended in the death of the experimenter, a new patent in Germany made a breakthrough possible. This discovery was registered to Graf von Zeppelin, but still, airships remained highly vulnerable: a sudden updraught of wind during the approach to the docking mast or the hangar could be enough to totally destroy the enormous thing, and many were lost without trace during storms. During the First World War, 96 zeppelins carried out 5,000 bombing raids on London. Of these 96, 72 were shot down or had an accident along the way. However, the considerable number of accidents did not decrease the euphoria. People gathered from afar to see a zeppelin in flight.

The concept was based on a light, load-bearing construction of aluminium girders and hoops covered with a silk fabric. Inside were cells holding the highly explosive hydrogen gas which provided lift and which, in the end, would prove fatal to the zeppelin. The first zeppelin, the LZ-I (Luftschiffsbau-Zeppelin-I) took off from Lake Constance on July 2, 1900. Subsequently, 129 more were built following the same principle, even after the death of Graf von Zeppelin in 1917. After the Allied ban on its building was lifted in 1928, the Graf Zeppelin (LZ-127) was built. It made a number of spectacular journeys over the North Pole region, the United States, Japan, the Middle East and, together with the Hindenburg (LZ-129), to South America. However it is the LZ-129 which continues to appeal to the imagination. This giant, 245 metres long and 45 metres in diameter, was filled with 200,000 cubic metres of hydrogen gas and took about 61 hours to transport 50 passengers to New York. It had luxury cabins and served six-course menus with generous supplies of champagne, while passengers enjoyed a breathtaking view over the ocean.

On May 6, 1937, after more than 58 successful flights between Germany and America, the LZ-129 exploded near New Jersey. In a matter of minutes all that was left was a smouldering heap of twisted aluminium and a departed dream. The scepticism generated by the spectacular pictures and the publicity the accident received brought the age of the airship to an abrupt end. The airplane, which for so long had been seen as inferior to the airship, but which was better equipped for mass transport, overtook the zeppelin for good.   R.K.

After the Hindenburg's (LZ-129) explosion during its landing near Lakehurst, New Jersey, dirigible airship construction was halted in Germany.

The Hindenburg (LZ-129), 1935.

In the early 1930s, things were not going well for American Airlines: their fleet of Fokker, Ford and Curtis machines made so much noise that their customers left them for the competition, the new Boeing 247. Douglas Aircraft was also developing an all-metal aircraft. American Airlines, however, found the DC-2 (Douglas Commercial-2) too small and instead ordered 20 of a larger version yet to be designed, which would seat 28 passengers. The DC-3 was developed under the leadership of Fred Stineman and rolled out of the hangar for its first test flight on December 17, 1935, the same day that the Wright brothers had made their first power-assisted flight 32 years earlier. In June 1936, the machine was flying a non-stop scheduled service from New York to Chicago. The aircraft was such a commercial success that for the first time a profit began to be made on passenger flights. (Previously this had only been possible with airmail flights.) Film stars used the DC-3 to commute between Hollywood and New York, and it also made flying attractive to the middle class.

Under the name "Dakota," the aircraft conquered the world. With some tens of thousands of units produced, more Dakotas were built than any other aircraft, past or present, and virtually every airline had them in service. It was a tireless workhorse in the Second World War, carrying troops and equipment to battlefields and dropping food to starving cities. Apart from the occasional museum demonstration flights, there are one or two planes still in service in remote areas of Africa and South America.

The Dakota had a new image in every respect. It represented not only the final stage of a technical development that had started some years earlier but also the apotheosis of the aesthetic ideas of the 1930s. It became the ultimate symbol of the modern age. Until that time, aircraft looked as if they had been put together from a big kit of separate parts such as wings, tailplanes, undercarriages and cabins, each constructed and mounted in its own individual way. They were wooden constructions, with linen or corrugated-metal plates stretched over them, and with walls incapable of withstanding any force without becoming seriously deformed. The Dakota, on the other hand, was a semi-monocoque construction in which curved metal skin made a significant contribution to the aircraft's strength and rigidity, so that it could be made much lighter. The fuselage and the wings merged smoothly into one another to form a single visual whole. This development took place in parallel with attempts in the motor industry to develop self-supporting bodywork.

Designers immediately recognized the Dakota as the sign of a new aesthetic, with its taut, brightly polished aluminium skin, swept-back wings, retractable undercarriage, emphatically streamlined shape, round nose, smooth nacelles and parabolic tailplane. As they saw it, the design found its justification in nature and turned out to be capable of enabling human beings to fly. In its praise, industrial designer Walter Dorwin Teague said that he knew of "no more exciting form in modern design"; he saw its clear organic shape as an example for the design of cars and many other products in daily use.   R.K.

The most popular airplane of all times, the DC-3, made flying accessible to the middle class.

CORD 810

Gordon Buehrig

An early, hand-crafted model of
the Cord 810 Convertible Sedan,
1936.

The Cord 810's role as a design icon was assured in 1951 when the Museum of Modern Art (MOMA) in New York selected it as one of the models to be exhibited in its "Eight Automobiles" show. The exhibition catalogue emphasized its aesthetic qualities, describing its appearance with a vocabulary more associated with art criticism than a description of a quintessentially functional product. MOMA's stress on the importance of styling was underlined in the text, suggesting that "each part is treated as an independent piece of sculpture, the whole collection being partially related by similar details for each unit."

Gordon Buehrig, the Cord 810's designer, was one of America's foremost automobile stylists of the interwar years, bringing his distinctive vision to three particular marques: Auburn, Cord and Duesenberg. Although several accounts have suggested that his ideas about modernity were significantly coloured by reading the 1927 English translation of Le Corbusier's *Vers une architecture* (1923), his outlook was also very much in tune with the futuristic visions of first-generation American industrial designers. These included Raymond Loewy and Norman Bel Geddes (1893–1958), both of whom devoted considerable energies to the field of transportation design as well as the contemporary American appetite for science fiction.

Buehrig's early career was relatively unremarkable but gathered pace after a move to the "Art and Color Section" at General Motors soon after it was launched in 1927. Working as an automobile designer under Harley Earl, the ambitious Buehrig remained at GM for only a few months and moved on swiftly to become chief body designer at the Stutz Motor Car Company in Indianapolis, where he designed bodies for the 1929 Stutz Le Mans sports cars. Scarcely had he settled his feet under the drawing board when he relocated once again to become chief designer at Duesenberg, where his most remarkable achievement was perhaps the Cord 810.

The low, high-powered 810 had front-wheel drive and was characterized by a sleek, aerodynamic profile with a minimum of superfluous detailing. One hundred hand-built, non-functional Cord 810s were displayed in late 1935 at the automobile shows in New York, Chicago and Los Angeles, attracting remarkable public attention as well as a flood of articles in the automobile press. Very much perceived as a "Car of the Future," a rush of advance orders ensued, and customers received bronze models of the car whilst awaiting delivery. This commenced in the spring of 1936 with the release of four models: the Westchester Sedan, the Beverly Sedan, the Convertible Coupé and the Convertible Sedan, retailing respectively at $1,995, $2,095, $2,145 and $2,195.

The design and manufacture of such a dramatically styled car was a remarkable achievement, particularly given the very modest budget devoted by the company to research and development. Possibly as a direct result, the Cord 810 was characterized by a certain amount of mechanical unreliability. Furthermore, the Depression years in the United States were not the most auspicious backdrop against which to market luxury cars. There were also growing financial problems at the Cord Corporation which, having been formed in 1929 through the bringing together of a wide range of transportation-related subsidiaries, eventually became a victim of the Depression when it was sold in 1937. This resulted in the bankruptcy of its automotive interests.   J.M.W.

The Cord's aerodynamic profile and protruding nose were standard characteristics.

(clockwise)
Cord 812 Supercharged Beverly
Sedan, 1937

Cord 810 Phaeton, 1936

Cord 810 Cabriolet, 1936

FIAT 500 TOPOLINO

Dante Giacosa

Dante Giacosa

1905	Born on January 3 in Rome
1922–27	Studies mechanical engineering at the Politecnico, Turin
1928–30	Designer for a car factory in Turin
1930	Joins Fiat, where initially he designs diesel engines (1930–32) and aircraft engines (1932–33)
1933	Becomes head of Fiat's private car division
1936	Fiat 500, the Topolino
1945–46	Cisitalia 202
1947–67	Professor at the University of Turin
1950–72	Designs more cars for Fiat: Fiat 1400 (1950), Fiat 8V (1952), Fiat 600 (1955), Fiat Nuova 500 (1957), Fiat 1800 (1959), Fiat 124 (1966), Fiat 125 (1967), Fiat 128 (1969), Autobianchi A112 (1969), Fiat 127 (1971) and Fiat 126 (1972)
1996	Dies on March 31 in Turin

Considerable efforts were made at Fiat, Italy, to produce a practical, well-designed, mass-produced and affordable car. It was this corporate ambition which Dante Giacosa and his design team at Fiat first brought to life in the design of the Type 500 which was to become known as the "Topolino" (the Italian word for Mickey Mouse). Its 569-cubic-centimetre engine gave a top speed of more than 50 miles per hour, returned more than 80 miles per gallon on flat roads and embraced many qualities of larger cars. The fact that it cost less than 10,000 lire made it widely affordable and it remained in production, with later variants, until 1955.

Like that of the later Morris Mini (1959; see p. 121), the Topolino's design was engineering-led. An innovatory chassis, independent front suspension, transverse springs and an extremely compact, four-cylinder engine were at its core, together with the positioning of the engine in front of the front axle and the radiator further back in the bonnet. Giacosa later stated that "the automobile will achieve its best results when its working conditions allow for the training of designers who combine technical knowledge with means of expression." In fact, the design of the Topolino embraced such a philosophy, bringing together a number of engineers and designers under the control of Giacosa, including engineers Virgilio Borsattino and Rodolfo Schaeffer (director of Fiat's body-styling department) respectively credited with the design of the engine and bodywork. The Topolino's compact styling had an aerodynamic quality, first seen in the larger Fiat 1500 of 1935—although such manifestations were much more restrained than contemporary American counterparts such as the Chrysler Airflow of 1934 and the radical format envisaged by Ferdinand Porsche for the German Volkswagen Beetle (1938; see p. 80). By the time Giacosa designed the New 500, launched in 1957, he had become an accomplished, all-round, designer, blending his many years experience of automotive engineering design with considerable panache as a body stylist.   J.M.W.

Giacosa also designed the Fiat Nuova 500, 1957.

Practical and affordable:
the Topolino made car ownership
possible for everyone.

SAVOY VASE

Alvar Aalto

Alvar Aalto

Alvar Aalto's most important contribution to glass design of the twentieth century is the so-called Savoy vase series from 1937. It was named after the Savoy Restaurant in Helsinki, which commissioned Aalto to design their interior as well as a series of vases. They were initially referred to as "Aalto Vases" or "Paris Objects," having been exhibited in the 1937 World Exposition in Paris. Aalto had already won first prize for his designs in a competition announced in 1936 by the glass manufacturer Karhula-Iittala.

Alvar Aalto and his wife Aino (1894–1949) had already participated in several glass competitions in the early 1930s—the first time in 1932, when Karhula-Iittala invited a number of designers to submit designs for new glass series. While the collaboration between Alvar and Aino Aalto as architects was so close that their individual contributions are often difficult to verify, Aino was free to pursue her own ambitions in product design. Aino and Alvar Aalto each delivered their own design, but only Aino won a second prize with her series in pressed glass called "Bölgeblick" (warped view). Alvar Aalto, on the other hand, was left empty-handed for his contribution entitled "Karhiit," a series of drinking glasses with two carafes intended for the Paimio Sanatorium that he had designed in 1929–33 (although one might wonder at the need for liquor, beer and whisky glasses in a sanatorium).

In 1933, the Riihimäki glassworks invited Alvar Aalto and nine other designers to participate in a competition for the Milan Trienniale. This time Aalto won a second prize. His design consisted of five glasses which, when stacked inside one another, combined into the shape of a flower. In the 1936 competition, the jury, which included many of Aalto's friends, awarded first prize to the five loosely sketched vases called "Eski måerinales skinnbuxa" (Eskimo girl's leather trousers), although production seemed problematic from a technical perspective. Aalto wanted to create the mould from sheet steel threaded through several steel rods attached to a firm base plate. The analogy to his experimental wood reliefs and to the frame of the Paimio chair was obvious; in the end, however, the moulds were carved from solid wood blocks.

The Savoy vases count among the earliest examples of organic form in design, a testimony to the various influences on Aalto. One of these was Finland's geography, charac-terized by mountains and lakes, and frequently captured in Aalto's architectural drawings. In addition, there was his familiarity with Surrealist art, which he incorporated into his wood reliefs, as well as his friendship with the sculptor Alexander Calder (1898–1976). Japanese art, to which Aalto was exposed through his contact with the Japanese consul in Helsinki, may also have played a role. In any case, the Savoy vase, still in production today, is Aalto's most popular glass design, although he never received a single penny for it aside from the 1937 prize money.   J.St.

The edges of Aalto's vases are reminiscent of the shorelines of Finland's many lakes.

Aalto's design sketches for the Finnish Glass Manufacturers competition.

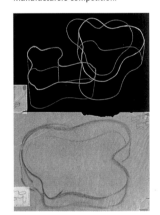

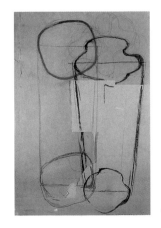

MINOX CAMERA

Walter Zapp

Walter Zapp

1905   Born on September 4 in Riga, Latvia

1922–24   Studies photography in Reval (now Tallinn) under the photographer Walter Lemberg

1932   With his friend Richard Jürgens, sets up a company to supply photographic equipment

1934–36   Develops the Minox camera

1938   The Minox camera is put into production by the Valsts Elektrotechniska Fabrika (VEF), Riga

1941–45   After the VEF factory is annexed by the AEG as a spoil of war, Zapp is employed by AEG's research department in Berlin

1945–48   Employed by the Ernst Leitz optics factory, Wetzlar; founds Minox GmbH with Jürgens

1948–50   Employed as chief designer and technical director of the newly opened Minox factory in Heuchelheim

1950   Leaves Minox factory after a commercial dispute with one of the company's financial backers

1996   Leica takes over the Minox company; they hire Zapp as a design consultant

Film still from *The Falcon and the Snowman*, 1984.

It was part of the standard equipment for secret agents and spies. Countless novels and movies (Canaris, James Bond) elevated the spy camera to unexpected fame. Any story set in the Cold War years was unthinkable without it. But crowned heads, too, preferred the miniature camera—naturally in a gilded version befitting their status. For all that, one quickly forgets that the Minox camera represents one of the most important milestones in the history of photography.

The muddled history of the Minox began in the 1930s in the Baltic region, not in Riga, Latvia, its inventor's birthplace, but in Reval (today Tallinn), where Walter Zapp, who had come to photography by a circuitous route, settled. In 1932, he founded a company for the development of medium-format cameras together with Richard Jürgens. When they ran into difficulties in producing their first camera, Zapp convinced his partner that a miniature camera would be much more likely to succeed—a project which had interested him for several years. He used a wood block measuring 12.5 by 28 by 75 millimetres as the smallest scale model to test the desired format for a hand- and pocket-sized camera. Next, he tried to adapt the required technology to the external, ideal image. In the interest of simple and expedient handling, for example, he omitted the diaphragm, superfluous at any rate because of the small dimension of the lens and its increased range of depth of focus. All that was necessary was a feature for adjusting the exposure, since distance only had to be measured with great precision in close-ups. When the preliminaries were completed—the final sectional drawing in colour is dated August 16, 1935—they were ready to create the first prototype. The greatest challenge was locating an appropriate lens, since few manufacturers in the Baltic region were equipped to produce one. Financially, too, the founding partners had reached their limit, and so they sought out a third partner. After several rejections from Western firms, Agfa among others, a suitable partner was found in 1936 in the state-run factory for radios and electrical equipment in Riga, VEF (Valsts Elektrotechniska Fabrika).

Changes in the picture format from 6.5 by 9 millimetres to 8 by 11 millimetres and other modifications delayed the market release date of the Minox until April 12, 1938. The positive reception and initial sales successes were abruptly slowed down by the outbreak of the Second World War, although production continued even under Soviet occupation. After the end of the war, the company started up again in the West with American support. In September 1945, Zapp and Jürgens founded the company Minox GmbH, Wetzlar, with the goal of developing an improved Minox. The cigar group Rinn and Cloos, Heuchelheim joined as partners. After initial successes, a rift occurred between Zapp and the rest of the board. Without the true designer or, rather, inventor, the company launched a big splash in 1958 with the Minox B, an upgraded successor to the original Minox, of which they manufactured nearly 400,000 models. Over time, many technical improvements were introduced. But the shape, unusually long with rounded edges, so instrumental in establishing the camera as a design classic, would remain largely unchanged for decades.   J.St.

(from top to bottom)
The first Minox prototype

The "Riga" Minox, 1938–43

The Minox A, the first micro or candid camera manufactured in Germany, 1948.

Original size of the
Minox, barely larger than
a cigarette lighter.

Designed in the 1930s,
the Hardoy chair became a cult
object in the 1950s and remains
modern to this day.

HARDOY CHAIR

Jorge Ferrari-Hardoy, Juan Kurchan
and Antonio Bonet

This simple, practical and effective chair, fabricated from metal rods and a canvas or leather "slung" seat, has become a celebrated design icon. Designed by three Argentinian architects called Gruppo Austral, who had worked under Le Corbusier in 1937, the chair clearly drew inspiration from earlier European precedents, most notably a foldaway wooden and canvas chair created by Joseph Beverly Fenby, a British engineer, in the mid-1850s (but not patented until 1877). Fenby's lightweight, practical and easily transported prototype was favoured by British army officers as well as many others interested in leisure pursuits. From the mid-1890s, it began to be produced in large quantities, by which time Fenby had sold the rights to French and Italian manufacturers, the latter marketing it as the "Tripolina" chair. However, in the United States it was known as the "Gold Medal No. 4" and was mass produced by the Gold Medal Company, Wisconsin, a manufacturer of folding and camping furniture.

Having been a prizewinner in an Argentinian furniture competition, the "Hardoy" chair (also known as the "Butterfly" chair) came to the attention of a key figure in the promotion of the exhibition series "Good Design in North America" (1950–55), Edgar Kaufmann Jnr. He purchased two of the first of such chairs to be imported to the United States. John McAndrew, a colleague of Kaufmann and Curator of Architecture at the Museum of Modern Art in New York, drew the chair to the attention of Clifford Pasco of Artek-Pasco. As a result, Pasco's company manufactured around 1,500 units prior to American involvement in the Second World War.

After the war, Hans Knoll of Knoll Associates (a leading furniture production and promotion company founded in 1946 in the United States) became involved with marketing the Hardoy chair, selling it under a royalty agreement with its principal designer. Its elegant appearance, simplicity of construction and level of comfort had endeared it to Knoll. Together with his wife Florence, he believed firmly in the patronage of talented designers whose products not only epitomized excellence and innovation but were committed to what became the Knoll company maxim: "Good design is good business." However, the chair's ease of construction and the relative cheapness of the materials from which it was fabricated meant that it soon was very widely copied, so much so that Knoll found it necessary to file a lawsuit against imitators. It became an important test case with implications for the design profession regarding definitions of originality of concept. However, Knoll had to accept defeat after it had been clearly established that the Hardoy design was itself closely derived from a number of precedents, even if fashioned from steel rods rather than the wooden skeletal components used in nineteenth-century precedents.

Variants of the design have sold internationally in the millions since the late 1930s, having a particular vogue during the 1950s when they were to be found in the offices of many designers, architects and other professionals with a commitment to a modern aesthetic. The Hardoy chair is also included in many major international collections of furniture around the world.   J.M.W.

VOLKSWAGEN BEETLE

Ferdinand Porsche

Ferdinand Porsche

1875	Born on September 3 in Mattersdorf near Reichenbach, Bohemia
1897	Patent registered for an electrical hub motor
1900	Presents electric automobile at the World Exposition in Paris
1906	Employment at Austro-Daimler-Motoren KG, Bierenz
1910	Success with an aerodynamically shaped automobile constructed by Austro-Daimler
1916–22	General director of Austro-Daimler
1923–29	Changes to Daimler-Motoren AG in Untertürkheim
1929–30	Works for Steyr-Werke AG
1931	Owns engineering office in Stuttgart; development of the Zündapp Type 12
1932	Presents a memorandum to the Ministry of Finance concerning the construction of a compact automobile
1933	Develops the Type 32 for NSU (first test drive in 1934)
1935	First driveable prototype of a Volkswagen Beetle
1939	Begins construction of military vehicles, including the "Tiger" tank
1947	Begins construction of the Porsche 356 sports car
1951	Dies on January 30 in Stuttgart

In January 1934, after having developed a number of experimental cars for Zündapp and NSU, all of which were intended for mass production, Ferdinand Porsche made a proposal, complete with sketches, for the development of a mass-produced *Volkswagen*—a people's car. His proposal opened with a reference to the *Volksempfänger* (People's Radio, 1933; see p. 56), a radio that anyone could afford and which had recently appeared on the market.

The contours of the later Volkswagen are clearly visible in the first sketches, which appeared as early as April. In June, Porsche was ordered by the government to develop a national car, "in order to promote car ownership in Germany. . . and to advance the welfare of the German empire." In 1938, after the development of various prototypes and arduous test drives all over Europe, the design was ready for production. A factory was built in Wolfsburg specifically for this purpose, and in that same year the *New York Times* mockingly named the car the "Beetle." At the beginning of 1939, the car was exhibited to the public in Berlin under the name "KdF" (Kraft durch Freude [Strength through Joy]) and people were able to acquire one by means of a savings-stamp system. In September, however, production was halted by the outbreak of war, and none of the more than 300,000 subscribers ever received a KdF or their money back.

Production was restarted by the British Army in 1945 as a way of stimulating employment, and the operation rapidly returned to German hands. In the 1950s, the Beetle was the symbol of German reconstruction and the mobility of the new urban middle class.   R.K.

Compact and economical: explore the world with a Beetle.

Cover to the advertising brochure, *Dein KdF-Wagen.*

In 1934, Citroën was taken over by the tyre manufacturer Michelin. Pierre Boulanger, a designer of inexpensive working-class housing, was given the order to get Citroën restarted. In 1935, he launched an idea for a car for the French farmer and his family, to replace the horse and cart. Ten thousand farmers, from all parts of the French countryside, were asked what sort of car they envisaged, what they would want to transport and over what distances. The engineer Maurice Brogly was given the order to design a kind of umbrella on four wheels, in which two farmers, in clogs, could be comfortably transported over the worst possible roads, with a sack of potatoes, a small cask of wine and a bucket of eggs, without breaking the eggs!

By 1937, there were 20 test models on the road, with bodies made of corrugated aluminium adapted from the German Ju-52 aircraft. The first model rolled off the production line the day before war broke out. Production was halted, and it was not until the 1948 "Salon d'Automobile" in Paris that the 2CV model—known as "Deux Chevaux" (two horses)—entered the market.

The 2CV, by now manufactured in steel plate, was at first only required to transport farmers, country doctors and midwives, but very soon the cheeky, wobbly vehicle became a craze for young families. In the 1960s, the car, intended for use in the country, became the means of transport that expressed the lifestyle of the young urban intellectual and the alternative scene of artists and hippies.   R.K.

Pierre Boulanger

1885   Born on March 10
        Studies architecture
1905   Contact begins with the Michelin family
1918   Designs housing for Michelin workers
1935   Director at Citroën following Michelin's
        acquisition of the company in 1934
1936   Commissioned by Pierre Michelin to
        construct a compact automobile,
        together with the engineer Maurice Brogly
        (later, André Lefebvre)
1938   General Director at Citroën after the
        death of Pierre Michelin
1950   Dies on November 11

Cult car: Deux Chevaux was one of the most successful French cars in the history of Europe.

PARKER 51 FOUNTAIN PEN

Kenneth Parker, Ivan D. Tefft, Marlin Baker and Joseph Platt

Promoted as "a pen from another planet" and "ten years ahead of its time" this sleek, aerodynamic design with its distinctive hooded nib was the result of a research programme which was completed in 1939. Introduced to commemorate the fifty-first anniversary of the Parker Company in the United States, it became one of the best-selling models (over 120 million sold) in Parker's history. Widely acknowledged as one of the best-designed consumer products of the century, the Parker 51 was featured in the book *Vision in Motion* (1946) by László Moholy-Nagy, a leading modernist and former teacher at the Bauhaus who had moved to the United States in 1937 at the invitation of Walter Gropius. The famous, elegant, arrow-shaped clip was originally designed for the 1933 Parker "Vacumatic" pen by Joseph Platt, a New York artist.

However, the Parker 51 not only looked good and was designed around ergonomic principles but also incorporated a number of technological advances which affected its performance. It was produced to very high levels of precision, and the internal barrel was fabricated from Lucite, a material highly resistant to the corrosive effects of a new, quick-drying ink (High Velocity 51). This ink had been developed by the Parker Company during the 1930s and enabled the folding and placing in envelopes of written material with a minimum of delay or the customary smudging. The filling system itself initially derived from the highly successful mechanism first presented to the public in the Parker Vacumatic, but was replaced in 1948 by an aeromatic system, siphon-based and fabricated from metal and Plexiglas.

The total development programme of the Parker 51 is reputed to have cost over $250,000: prior to its official release in the United States in 1941, at a retail price of $12.50, the pen was tested in Venezuela and Brazil over a two-year period. The pen came of age commercially after the Second World War, in the concluding stages of which General Dwight D. Eisenhower signed the Armistice to end the war on the European front with his Parker 51. In 1946 alone, over 5 million of them were manufactured.

The Parker 51 inspired a number of imitators, although few managed to capture the suave elegance of its design. An exception to this was Marcello Nizzoli's "Aurora 88," produced in Italy from 1947 onwards, with its striking gold-plated cap and black plastic reservoir.

J.M.W.

The arrow-shaped clip of the Vacumatic fountain pen (far left) reappeared in the design of the Parker 51.

Advertisements for the Vacumatic and Parker 51 fountain pens from the 1940s.

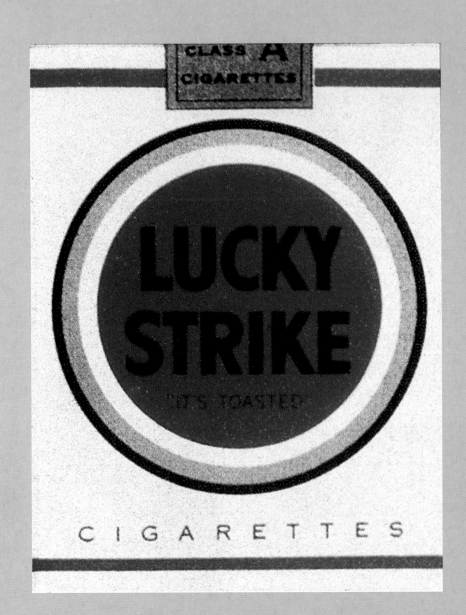

The Lucky Strike brand, which appeared on the U.S. market in 1916, is inseparably linked with the rise of the cigarette as a mass stimulant. At the beginning of the twentieth century, the cigarette was still an exotic item, reserved for artists and other eccentric types. In 1913, Camel came up with the first modern cigarette, in which Turkish and Virginia tobaccos were blended in such a way as to allow smokers to inhale without coughing. Shortly afterwards Chesterfield brought out a comparable mixture.

In the 1930s, thanks to unusual forms of promotion and advertising, Lucky Strike, a latecomer, became a market leader. The aim of their advertising campaign was to convince women that smoking was good for them and that modern women smoked in public, since the number of women smokers was below that of men. The approach was new, but their packaging had remained unchanged since its first introduction. Raymond Loewy, a fashionable and publicity minded designer, was severely critical of everything not designed by himself, and so of the packaging of Lucky Strike. In the autumn of 1940, George Washington Hill, president of the American Tobacco Company, charged unannounced into Loewy's office. After proving his good taste by displaying his expensive Cartier braces, he challenged Loewy to a $50,000 bet that he could not think up a better style of packaging. Loewy first responded by showing him his own handmade Cartier braces, then vowed that in no more than a few hours he could produce a new design. The two men immediately recognized one another as kindred spirits and quickly became friends. One fine spring day Loewy made one or two sketches and half a dozen models which he personally found very satisfactory. Only after Hill himself had spent a few hours at Loewy's desk, fruitlessly cutting and pasting, was Loewy's design put into production. Since then it has remained virtually unchanged.

What Loewy did was replace the muddy green colour with a brilliant white background. This time he put the red circle, which originally appeared only on the front, on both the front and the back of the pack. The inevitable pieces of text, which nobody ever read, were tucked away on the sides of the pack. This arrangement ensured that the pack would always lie with the red circle trademark facing up, and that there would be no visual interference from any text. The new packaging was startlingly different from the old one. Instead of an old-fashioned, rather dingy pack, all at once it acquired a totally modern aura. The bright red and brilliant white suggested freshness and, more particularly, hygiene—an aspect that at the time was emphatically linked with smoking. An alternative explanation for the choice of white was that green pigment had been declared a strategic material and so was no longer available for civilian use.   R.K.

Raymond Loewy
Biography, see p. 60

The dark green Lucky Strike package seemed old-fashioned.

Loewy's modified design gave Lucky Strike a new image and increased sales.

Advertisement for Lucky Strike cigarettes, ca. 1950.

WURLITZER JUKEBOX 1015

Paul Fuller

Paul Fuller

1897	Born on January 5 in Switzerland
ca. 1920	Emigrates to the United States
1920–25	Works on a farm in Wyoming
ca. 1925	Joins the Marshall Field & Co. department store in Chicago, where he is responsible for layout and product presentation
1933	Designs a presentation on the theme "Black Forest" for Chicago's Century of Progress Exposition
1935–48	Chief designer for the Rudolf Wurlitzer Company in North Tonawanda, New York; during this period designs 17 jukeboxes for the company including the models 312 (1936), 1015 (1946) and 1100 (1947)
1939	Designs a presentation on the theme "Alpine Village" for the New York World's Fair
1949	Opens his own design office in Oneida, New York, where he mainly designs furniture and pianos
1951	Dies on March 29 in Buffalo, New York

Film still from *In This Our Life*, 1942, starring Bette Davis.

After the end of the Second World War, the Wurlitzer 1015 proved extremely popular, with sales of over 56,000 in the first 18 months of its release onto the market. It became the most successful jukebox ever with its eloquent arched top and styling details which incorporated animated bubble tubes, revolving colour columns and a visible record-changing mechanism. Paul Fuller was perhaps the most influential designer to work for Wurlitzer which, by the 1940s, was the largest and best-known manufacturer of jukeboxes.

Wurlitzer was established in the late nineteenth century as a manufacturer of pianos, soon moving into coin-and-slot phonographs and later into cinema organs. In the 1930s, following the Wall Street Crash and diversification into refrigerators and furniture, the company emerged as the market leader of jukeboxes, easily outstripping the other three manufacturers with which it comprised the Big Four: Seeburg, AMI and Rock-Ola. The designer Paul Fuller played a leading role in Wurlitzer's success, exploring a vibrant aesthetic vocabulary characterized by "light-up" cabinets with brightly coloured plastic elements—very far removed from the heavy and often prosaic styling of many radio consoles. This emphasis on colour and light (which was given additional interest through variable effects produced by the incorporation of "bubble tubes," polarized films and filters) became an essential ingredient in the sensory appeal of jukeboxes. The arch-top format which Fuller so warmly embraced in many of his designs, such as the Model 1015, may well have been influenced by the styling of the Seeburg Model Q jukebox of 1937 and first appeared in the Wurlitzer range in the Model 750 of 1941. Amongst the range of other well-known jukeboxes designed by Fuller was the imposing and ostentatious Model 850 of 1941, "The Peacock." A veritable *tour de force* of visual exuberance, it incorporated a translucent, back-lit heraldic shield, surrounded by metal grille and illuminated plastic panels, with variable lighting setting off a central peacock motif.

Described at the time of its launch by Wurlitzer as "the only super deluxe phonograph in the industry," the Model 850 was a classic production of the Golden Age of jukebox design which lasted from approximately 1937 to 1948. It also embraced many of the enduring qualities which distinguished the more adventurous designs of the period from their prosaic radio console and gramophone antecedents: it was large, ostentatious and rich with visual interest, utilizing illuminated plastic panels.

The Model 1015 very closely accords with the public's dominant image of the jukebox at the height of its social and cultural significance. As with so many other arenas of design in the 1980s, nostalgia and heritage played a role in the audio industry. The Wurlitzer "One More Time CD" jukebox adopted the Model 1015 casing, but was, in fact, a microprocessor-controlled compact disc changer and player. It also borrowed many other traits from its ostentatious forebears: the rotating colour columns, rounded arch top and trademark bubble tubes, all of which contributed to an archetypal vision of the American jukebox.   J. M.W.

(right)
The Model 1015 from 1946: lavish decoration, rotating light columns and glorious colours are the trademarks of Fuller's designs.

Wurlitzer Model 750 (top) and the Model 850 from 1941.

VESPA MOTOR SCOOTER

Corradino d'Ascanio

Corradino d'Ascanio

1897	Born on February 1 in Popoli, Italy
1910–14	Studies mechanical engineering at the Politecnico, Turin
1915–18	Serves as pilot in the Italian Air Force
1918	Designs various aircrafts for the Pomilio aircraft factory in Indianapolis, Indiana
1920–33	Returns to Italy and works as a freelance engineer for various industrial organizations
1930	After five years' experimentation, constructs the world's first working helicopter
1933–40	Designs aircraft engines with variable-pitch propellers for Piaggio's aircraft engine division in Finale Ligure and Pontedera
1945–46	Various prototypes for Piaggio's Vespa scooter (in cooperation with Enrico Piaggio)
1946–64	Develops a series of different Vespa models, including Vespa 98 (1946), Vespa 125 (1948, 1951, 1953, 1958, 1960), Vespa 150 GS (1955), Vespa 150 (1959) and Vespa 50 (1964)
1949	Helicopter PD-3
1952	Helicopter PD-4
1981	Dies in Pisa

The Vespa motor scooter, designed by Piaggio's chief engineer, Corradino d'Ascanio, in 1946, stands out as one of the most innovative pieces of transportation design in the twentieth century. Its originality lies not only in its striking, modern-looking form and revolutionary statement about how to move large numbers of people from A to B but also in its strongly symbolic impact on early post-war Italy.

To start with the last, the Vespa scooter symbolized the post-war, post-fascist democracy that was Italy in the years after 1945. Replacing the bicycle—the key transportation object of the working man and woman before the war—its presence in the narrow backstreets of Italy's cities, buzzing along as its name "wasp" implied, stood for the new mobilized society which had passed through the ravages of fascism and war and survived to tell the tale. From 1915 onwards, the Piaggio engineering works had manufactured airplanes, but following wartime bombing, the firm's director, Enrico Piaggio, had decided to concentrate on the production of a cheap, reliable transport object which was easy to drive and to maintain. The motor-scooter that resulted was dramatically different from other types which had existed hitherto. Instead of creating a motorized version of the foot-powered scooter, d'Ascanio brought his experience with helicopter and aircraft design to bear on the project, resulting in the emergence of an object which combined helicopter body construction with a two-wheeled, road-bound mode of transport. The "mono-coque" construction of the Vespa meant that the curved, metal body-shell was at one with its structure. This was not merely a question of hanging metal elements onto a pre-existing frame: the result was a "space-age" bulbous object which owed much to the visual language of American streamlining. But unlike streamlined American cars, however, the Vespa had no extraneous surface detailing—no chromed metal "speed lines" for example. Like a number of its famous Italian design neighbours from these years—Pininfarina's Cisitalia car; Marcello Nizzoli's "Lexicon 80" typewriter for Olivetti, and Gio Ponti's "La Pavoni" coffee-machine—this was a stripped-down version of streamlining which had a strongly sculptural appeal. The Vespa soon became a familiar appendage of the post-war Italian environment, taking men to work and women shopping. Such was its appeal that it became an accessory to Britain's youth culture in the 1960s. It survives today as a lasting image of twentieth-century modernity.

P.S.

Inexpensive, reliable and low in maintenance, the Vespa was, and still is, popular with young and old.

A prototype of the MP5 Paperino, 1943–4

The Vespa MP6, 1946 never went into mass production.

The Vespa 125 was launched in 1948.

The Vespa 150 GS.

The first Vespa sports model, the 150 GS, was capable of accelerating to 100 kilometres per hour and sold in the millions.

Tupperware Home Parties

Earl S. Tupper first worked as a chemist at DuPont in the 1930s before setting up his own business. Around 1940, he heard about the new material polyethylene, a thermoplastic developed in England that was used to protect electric wire. Most plastics at the time were duroplastics, that is, materials pressed under heat and stress, such as Bakelite, galalith and ebonite. Tupper approached the DuPont management in 1942 and presented them with his idea of new soft plastic household containers. As a team, Tupper-DuPont succeeded in developing a finer version of the new plastic, which Tupper called "Poly-T"—"Material of the Future." They also developed a new injection moulding process.

In 1946, immediately after the end of the war-driven economy, Tupper Plastics launched its assortment of food containers. Soft plastic made it easy to preserve the contents in an airtight container. When the lid was closed over the patented rim and gently pressed down, a negative pressure resulted inside the container, and the external air pressure sealed the lid tightly around the edge. Tupper was confident that his invention would conquer the market; he spoke of the "Tupperization" of America. Although plastics spread quickly as a booming new industry, Tupperware was soon taken up by the public—the majority of DuPont's polymer production went to Tupper in 1950. The products were excitingly novel: unscented, unbreakable, solid, colourful and inexpensive. Until then, plastics had been predominantly a replacement material for more expensive materials which they tried to imitate, such as costly mother-of-pearl, but now they went beyond imitation and revealed themselves in fresh colours with new qualities which ensured their position in the marketplace.

In 1951, Tupper made an astonishing decision: he withdrew his products from all retail stores and began to sell them exclusively through so-called Tupperware Parties, organized by travelling saleswomen in private home settings. The sales representative Brownie Wise, who had been very successful with this approach, had convinced him to take this step. Now Tupper achieved a much more direct sales setting than what was available in any store. Potential shoppers gathered information about the product through demonstrations and were able to verify its use by handling it themselves. This method of sales and distribution, still practised today, brought Tupper surprising and lasting success, and Wise was appointed vice-president, a position which she held for many years.   C.L.

Earl S. Tupper

1907	Born in Farnumsville, Massachusetts
1942	Discovers a process for casting polyethylene as a chemist for DuPont in Massachusetts
1945	Founds the Tupper Plastic Factory
1946	Begins distribution of Tupperware through "home parties" in the United States
1958	Sells the company to the Rexall Drug Company; retires to Costa Rica
1960	Distribution of Tupperware begins in Great Britain
1983	Dies in Costa Rica

Since the 1950s, Tupperware parties have been an ingenious sales strategy.

(below, left to right)
The "Picnic Set," launched in the 1950s, made the hearts of true Tupperware fans beat faster. Since the 1960s, one of the most popular products has been the "Magic Bowl."

ARABESQUE TABLE

Carlo Mollino

Mollino took part in international car races, alpine ski races and flying competitions.

Carlo Mollino

Reducing Carlo Mollino's contribution to the history of design to one single piece of furniture can only do justice to his achievement as architect, designer and photo artist when contextualized within the totality of an impressive oeuvre that encompasses nearly all artistic disciplines. Carlo Mollino is one of the few protagonists of his trade who stands for a repertoire of forms, a deep experiential and intellectual understanding of design that has always resisted traditional views and conformist thinking.

Born in Turin in 1905, Mollino designed and built alpine ski resorts, racetracks, theatres and drive-ins, as well as administration and apartment buildings after completing his studies in architecture. He created film and theatre sets, developed unique patent-worthy systems for exhibitions and supporting frameworks, and constructed airplanes and racing cars, among others a twin-engined "Bisiluro" which took part in the 24-hour race at Le Mans and set a track record that held for two years.

He achieved fame, however, through his many private and public interiors and for the furniture he designed to accompany them. All are remarkable for their sweeping visual range, revealing an ability to adapt to a wide variety of requirements in terms of function, structure and especially ambience. While the boudoirs, created to satisfy the designer's personal artistic obsessions, are imbued with a sultry decadence in their surrealistic mannerism, his furnishings—bunk beds, desks and dining tables and, not least, chairs designed for offices, galleries and urban apartments—display an inventive passion that is sometimes inspired by bionics. But Mollino was not only capable of dissecting forms, he also knew how to synthesize such diametrically opposed aspects as construction and decoration within a single design.

One of the best-known examples is his "Arabesque" coffee table, of which he created several versions for different commissions in the early 1950s. More than any other piece of furniture, this table demonstrates Mollino's search for a determinedly artistic expression not only through integration but also through optimizing structural material characteristics. The chair's S-bend laminate base and glass plates fulfil static as well as decorative functions. Both materials are used in accordance to their specific characteristics: rigidity, bendability and formability. Thus, this table is not only a masterpiece of artistic creation but also an embodiment of ingenious design.   V.A.

Mollino designed the first Arabesque table for the living room of the Casa Orenga in Turin.

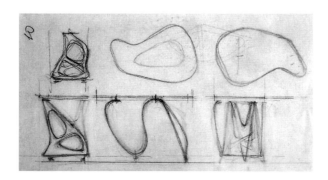

Studies by Mollino for the Arabesque series.

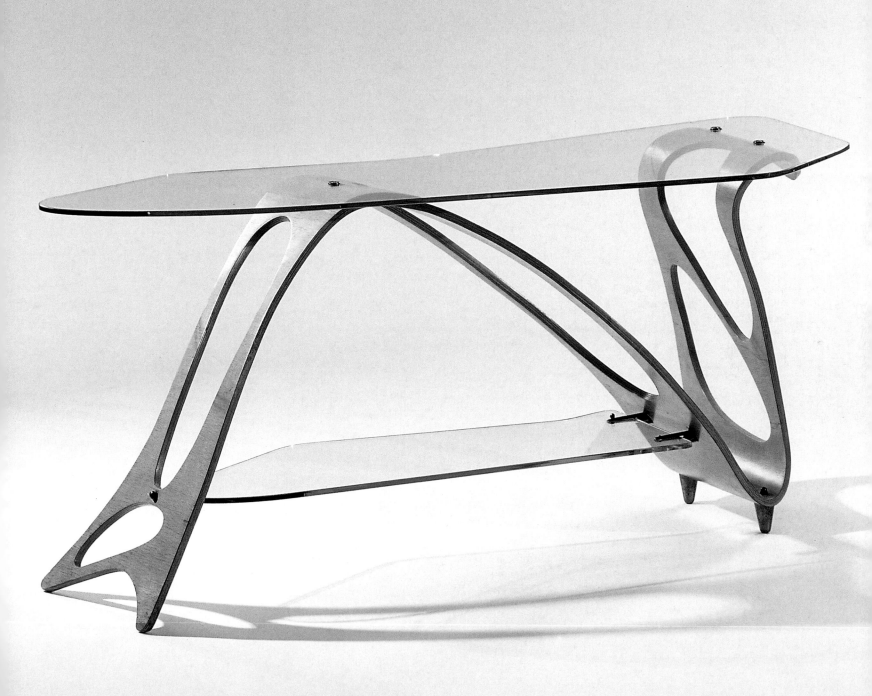

UNIVERS FONT

Adrian Frutiger

Adrian Frutiger

1928	Born on May 24 in Unterseen, Switzerland
1944–48	Apprenticeship as a typesetter, Interlaken
1948–51	Studies at the School for Arts and Crafts, Zurich with Walter Käch and Alfred Willimann
1952	Moves to Paris; head designer at the Deberny & Peignot type foundry
1952–60	Teaches at the Estienne School, Paris
1954–68	Teaches at the National School for Decorative Arts, Paris
1955	Méridien typeface
1962	Founds his own atelier with André Gürtler and Bruno Pfäffli, Arcueil, near Paris
1963–81	Consultant the design of typewriter fonts for IBM
1967	Serifa typeface
1968	Begins close collaboration with D. Stempel AG, Frankfurt am Main, that is continued with Linotype AG, Linotype Hell AG and Linotype Library
1973	The Optical Character Recognition-Class B (OCR-B) becomes an international, standard typeface
1975	Iridium typeface
1976	Develops Frutiger typeface from the information system for Charles de Gaulle Airport, Paris
1986	Receives the Gutenberg Prize from the city of Mainz
1992	Moves to Bremgarten, near Berne
1993	Grand Prix de la Culture Française

The aesthetic standards which would typify font in the twentieth century developed slowly over a long period of time. The first sans-serif fonts were designed circa 1810. They appeared cold, unfeeling, grotesque and were a complete failure both commercially and aesthetically. While attempts at new beginnings and new definitions were successfully implemented in the early 1930s in all other areas of design, typography continued to use an alphabet designed in 1896, the Akzidenz-Grotesque. Following experimental work at the Bauhaus and by the De Stijl movement, the conservative medium of type, until then defined in thought and form by influences dating back to the Renaissance, finally broke with the past and developed significant shapes applicable to the twentieth century. Since no text alphabet existed that could be adapted to include a wide range of typefaces, such as light-faced, bold, condensed, normal, italic, etc., and to provide a necessary typographical structure and formal unity, it was the custom—above all in the 1920s—to set words, lines and text individually in order to achieve a specific effect. These slightly awkward attempts led to the creation of the first alphabet that met modern requirements: Futura was developed and designed by Paul Renner from 1927 onwards. When political powers (especially in Germany) inhibited further growth in the area of new typography, work continued in Switzerland to perfect a font which would deliver a practical and internationally accepted typographical style for modern communication. This Swiss typography was created predominantly through a combination of Akzidenz-Grotesque normal and bold face. But its limitations were evident from the outset, and, after 1945, the idea caught on to create an alphabet based on modern forms, one that was capable of including an extensive and compatible alphabet family.

With Univers, Adrian Frutiger created the font of an era that integrated the innovations of Modernism up to 1950. It became an irreplaceable conceptual model for all other text alphabets. For the first time in the history of font design, the 21 Univers alphabets were planned and realized as a connected conceptual system. In blended applications, its letters always had the look of deriving from the same font family. This was feasible because of the minute calculation of stroke width and the relationship between stroke and the surrounding white space.

Although Helvetica, created from 1957 onwards, was more successful commercially and more widely spread, Frutiger's rigorous and visionary concept made Univers the most significant font of the century. Even today its appearance is fresh and contemporary, that is, timeless. Univers was modified in 1997 and expanded to 59 cuts to keep pace with the latest communication requirements.   F.F.

UNIVERS 39

UNIVERS 49

UNIVERS 59

UNIVERS 47

UNIVERS 48

UNIVERS 57

UNIVERS 58

UNIVERS 67

UNIVERS 68

UNIVERS 45

UNIVERS 46

UNIVERS 55

UNIVERS 56

UNIVERS 65

UNIVERS 66

UNIVERS 75

UNIVERS 76

UNIVERS 85

UNIVERS 86

UNIVERS 53

UNIVERS 63

UNIVERS 83

(right)
Frutiger's diagram of the
21 possible variations of the
Univers 55—derived by increasing
the stroke width of the letters
or by bolding them.
The first number refers to the
bolding (4 = light, 5 = roman,
6 = bold, etc.) and the second
to the width (7 = condensed,
5 = normal, 3 = extended, etc.)

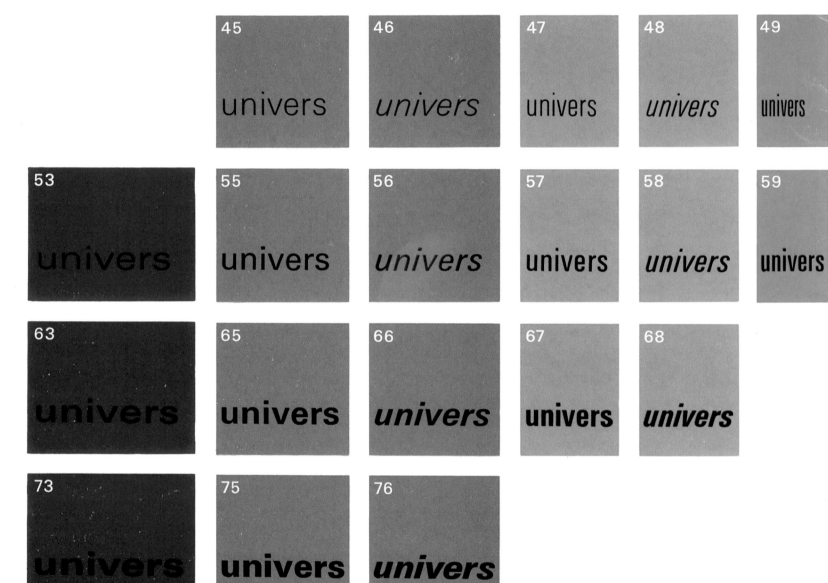

39 univers

45 univers
46 *univers*
47 univers
48 *univers*
49 univers

53 univers
55 univers
56 *univers*
57 univers
58 *univers*
59 univers

63 **univers**
65 **univers**
66 ***univers***
67 **univers**
68 ***univers***

73 **univers**
75 **univers**
76 ***univers***

83 **univers**

Proportion is key: Frutiger demonstrates with the letter "a" how optimal legibility can be achieved with lower case letters.

(left)
TWA Lockheed Super G
Constellation above New York.

In 1955, Lufthansa introduced
scheduled intercontinental
flights with the Lockheed Super
Constellation. The first regular
route was between Hamburg
and New York.

The Lockheed L1649 A Starliner of 1957 arguably represents the ultimate in piston-engined airliners, entering service only a few years before jet-powered Boeing 707s dominated those same air lanes. Its sleek lines and tri-tailed form derive from the Super G Constellation of 1955, the Super Constellation of 1951, and the famous 049 Constellation itself of 1939–43. For design aficionados, the 1951 Super Constellation is perhaps the most important of these: its compartmentalized interiors that divided the long fuselage into more intimate spaces were a trademark of noted industrial designer, Henry Dreyfuss. Though not the first airline design by Dreyfuss (see, for instance, his proposal in *Architectural Forum* [July 1944] to convert B-24 bombers into airliners), the Super Constellation was important because it led him to other airline commissions that range from the corporate imagery of American Airlines in the 1960s and 1970s to interiors of the turbo-prop Lockheed Electra of 1957. The Constellation itself, however, began life in 1939 as the result of Howard Hughes's requirements for a long-range, pressurized airliner for his airline, TWA. The distinctive, tri-tailed design provided by Lockheed was the work of the team of Hall Hibbard and Clarence "Kelly" Johnson (1910–1990). The latter was the chief designer and originator of many of Lockheed's famous planes of the 1930s to 1950s, from the twin-tailed P-38 Lightning to the P-80 Shooting Star, America's first operational jet fighter, to the famous U-2 spyplane. The name Constellation derives from the fact that the design incorporated so many tried-and-tested concepts from earlier Lockheed planes, that it was said to encompass an entire "constellation" of stellar ideas, though the plane is often affectionately called "Connie."

The model 049 Constellation made its first flight in 1943, the type being designated C-69 by the Army. Only 22 were used by them before the end of the war. Although Hughes's TWA ordered 40 of the planes in 1940, the initial post-war production went to TWA as well as Pan American, the latter inaugurating the first commercial service on January 20, 1946. The early model aircraft could hold some 43–60 people, depending upon the seating configuration, as well as 4 to 5 crewmembers. The "Connie" cruised at 265 miles per hour, with a top speed of some 370 miles per hour and a service altitude of up to 25,000 feet. And, on April 19, 1944, Howard Hughes himself piloted the second production model in a transcontinental, record-breaking flight from Burbank, California to Washington, D.C. in 6 hours and 57 minutes. It made transatlantic and cross-country flights a regular occurrence in the post-war era. After the Constellations' success with Pan Am and TWA, other airlines ordered them and their successors, the Super Constellation and Starliner. Beyond its impact on democratizing air transportation in the pre-jet era, the Constellation's tri-tail became its visual trademark. Some have said that this form, as well as the like-styled twin-tail of Lockheed's P-38, inspired car stylists at Cadillac in the early 1950s to shape their car's tail-lights in a similar way. More than 850 Constellations and their derivatives were built, though few are operable today. However, airplane aficionados of Save a Connie, Inc. have restored one of the Super G Constellations to its original appearance, flying it for air shows and reminding us all of the importance of this striking design.   J.Z.

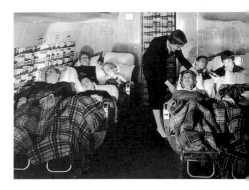

WOODEN TRAY

Tapio Wirkkala

Tapio Wirkkala

1915	Born on June 2 in Helsinki, Finland
1933–36	Trains as a sculptor at the Institute for Arts and Crafts, Helsinki
1947	Begins work for the Karhula-Iittala glassworks, for which he designs silverware, ceramics and lamps; works as a freelance designer on the side
1951	Finnish Pavilion at the ninth Milan Triennale
1951–54	Artistic director at the Institute for Arts and Crafts, Helsinki
1954	Finnish Pavilion at the tenth Milan Triennale
1955	Works for the Raymond Loewy Studio, New York
1956	Begins to work for Rosenthal, Selb
1958	Finnish Pavilion for the World Exposition in Brussels
1959–85	Works for Venini
1961	Made an honorary member of the Royal Society of Arts, London
1963	Designs "Puukko" knife for Hackman
1964	Named Royal Designer for Industry, London
1965	"Karelia" series of glasses
1972	Becomes a member of the Academy of Arts, London
1975	Honorary member of the industrial designers of the National Polytechnic Institute, Mexico City
1985	Dies on May 19 in Helsinki

In January 1952, the American magazine *House Beautiful* nominated Tapio Wirkkala's design of a wooden tray as the most beautiful object of 1951. It took the form of a tree leaf and was made by gluing together alternate layers of light and dark veneer, planing them at an angle and curving them at various points so that the individual layers of veneer could be seen on the surface. The carefully controlled curvature of the surface created a fluid pattern, evoking the veining of a leaf. Undoubtedly, many of the decisions on how the pattern should run were only made by instinct during the process of construction. Yet at the same time, the compelling repetition of the alternating shades of the different layers and the lack of any trace of hand or machine tooling gave the powerful impression that the design, structure and construction were so precisely thought out in advance that the outcome was completely predetermined. The perfection of the pattern was so obvious that one could hardly believe that it came as a surprise to its maker. A whole series could have been flawlessly reproduced simply by carefully following the design. This precise combination of feeling and intellect was captured in a razor-sharp contour of curves, blending to form the leaf of a tree in a way that could only be achieved by a sensitive hand. The tray expressed the erosion of the earth, the continuity and transience of the changing seasons.

Finnish design often expresses the visual strength of nature, though usually more indirectly than in these two blended impressions. The style is minimal, spare in its expression and use of material, with a cool subtlety and precision of line that reminds one of the purity of snow in great silent forests and the steel-blue, polar light falling on myriad frozen lakes. The controlled emotion of this style is appreciated all around the world and, in the 1930s, was associated with international ideas on modern design.

Finnish designers are also masters of an organic style based on a tradition of craft practised for generations, in small villages and farmhouses, by craftsmen who loved their tools and materials. This is much more lively and elegant and seems to have derived directly from observation of the living world—of moving leaves and the reflection of sunlight on the ripples in a river. This style of design comes from the soil and is charged with emotion and the promise of growth and renewal.

To Wirkkala, both forms of expression came as naturally as breathing and sight. During the long summer days, he would float by himself in his canoe over the quiet Finnish lakes, absorbing everything he saw. He would also spend long hours in his design studio and in workshops and factories, working on and reshaping the images and his materials until they achieved what he wanted to see. R.K.

Minimal form and materials: Wirkkala's leaf-shaped tray beautifully echoes nature.

ANT CHAIR
Arne Jacobsen

Arne Jacobsen

Arne Jacobsen's "Myren" (Ant) chair is one of a few furniture classics not distinguished by a dated, contemporary look. Instead, this exceptional design has become a symbol of time-lessness over the course of years, even decades. The chair is also extraordinarily versatile. More than any other, the Ant chair can be placed almost anywhere: in kitchens, canteens, offices, reception rooms and conference rooms. This is not only a result of its unpretentious image. It has none of the mannered theorism that characterizes so many of the rectangular modernist classics.

Jacobsen created the chair in 1952. Only after the first 200 models had withstood the wear and tear of use in the factory's cafeteria did manufacturer Fritz Hansen include the Ant chair in his production schedule. In the intervening years, over 5 million have been produced worldwide. The chair is available with three or four legs. The four-legged version, however, was introduced to the market only after the death of the designer. During his lifetime, Jacob-sen stubbornly resisted the creation of a four-legged version. The same is true of the now familiar range of colours. Jacobsen initially chose four different wood models and one version in black lacquer. To complement the Ant chair (model 3100), Jacobsen designed a series of variations in the 1950s, among them the notorious model 3107 (1955) that became (in)famous worldwide thanks to the scandalous 1963 Profumo affair involving a British government minister and playmate Christine Keeler. To Jacobsen's disappointment, the chair upon which Keeler posed was a mere copy of his original.

What all these variations had in common was the simple construction. All models consisted of two components: a seat and backrest formed from a piece of plywood and a three- or four-legged, slender, tubular-steel support structure or—as in the office version—a single column resting on five castors. This structure is attached to the seat in only one spot. The actual attachment is effected by three or four hard rubber blocks connected to the steel tubes. And yet the chair never gives the impression of being unstable or even fragile. On the contrary: the trapezoid layout of the construction of the chair promises solid stability. The essential component, however, the unobtrusively organic shape of the seat, promises one thing above all else: comfort.   V.A.

The successor to the Ant chair: the stackable chair (model 3107), stands on four legs.

Since the 1980s, the Ant chair has been available in 16 colours and several types of wood, manufactured by Fritz Hansen.

ROLODEX ROTARY CARD FILE

Arnold Neustadter

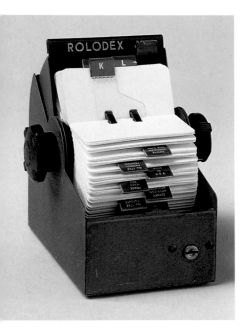

An early design of the Rolodex
featured a lockable box, late 1940s.

Arnold Neustadter (1910–1996) was an inventor and designer of "dexes"—as he called them. His corporation—appropriately called Zephyr American—aimed to speed up and streamline office efficiency. In the 1930s and 1940s, Neustadter first gave America the "Autodex," a flat phone directory which pops up at the desired letter and which is still manufactured today. Then came the "Swivodex," a spill-proof inkwell. There was also the "Clipodex," a writing pad which clipped onto a secretary's knees. But then he modified the already existing "Wheeldex" to come up with the classic Rolodex® Rotary Card File, which hit the market in the early 1950s.

The Rolodex made Neustadter rich. He sold his company in 1960, and it has been bought and sold several times since. In the 1980s, over 32 card file models were available (one of the models, the "6035X," boasted 3 wheels, held up to 6000 cards and featured "Torque-A-Matic" knobs to help you get to the right card more quickly!). In the 1990s, the manufacturer claimed that it sold 10 million Rolodexes annually. "It's turned out to be bigger than I ever thought it would be," Neustadter said mildly 40 years later.

Fittingly enough, Neustadter was an office-manager type, efficient and detail oriented. But he was also interested in the arts: he collected glass paperweights and modern art. The Rolodex, his own masterpiece, is more than good, functional design. It is simplicity made elegant: its shiny, tubular-steel frame—today manufactured in lightweight aluminium—heavy but streamlined, sprung forward and back into perfect balance, is reminiscent of the tubular-steel cantilever chair designs by Mies van der Rohe of 1927 (see p. 45). The Rolomatic® cylinder, the cradle for the notecards, dials 360 degrees easily to the desired letter or card and is held there by a ball-bearing clutch mechanism, which clicks smoothly and solidly into place. The Rolodex's no-nonsense, speedy looks and performance is American high modern, and it has lasted astonishingly well. How many other design triumphs of the 1950s, whether a finned automobile or a B-52, don't today look dated?

The Rolodex has also ridden the computer revolution like a surfer on a wave—a fact which has surprised many observers—and computer and hand-held electronic organizers even cater to the Rolodex, offering software that allows you to print address information onto pre-slotted Rolodex notecards. Some attribute the Rolodex's continuing appeal and success to its social cachet. Journalists, publicists and agents impress clients with the size—or number—of their Rolodexes or by leaving it open at an impressive card. In the 1960 film *The Apartment*, Jack Lemmon plays Bud Baxter, who climbs the executive ladder by making good use of his Rolodex—the symbol of the idea that "it's not what you know but who you know that counts." Design historian Phil Patton, in his book *Made in the USA* (1992), offers another explanation. He speculates that in the age of flat, high-tech computer screens we "hunger for meaning, solidity, texture in objects." The Rolodex certainly is a device that we enjoy touching, feeling, spinning; it requires the human touch to function and, like a weathered photo album, it documents as well as facilitates human contact.   J.C.M.

Function and form
are a dynamic duo
in the Rolodex design.

Climbing to the top with the
help of a well-sorted Rolodex:
Jack Lemmon in *The Apartment*
(1960).

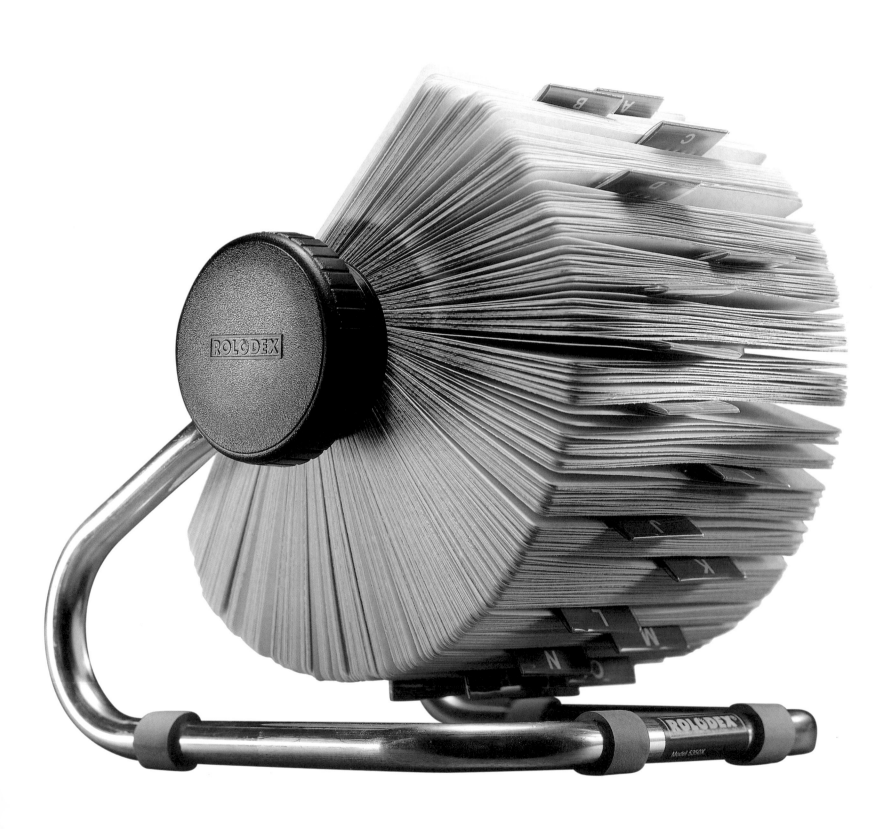

Great design variations: the original 1953 model, roof down and hard top; in the background, prototype models for a fastback coupé and a stationwagon.

In 1917, the originally Swiss (Louis) Chevrolet offered his make to General Motors, which would hold over 50 per cent of the market share after the Second World War. GM was actively investing in the future with so-called Autoramas, a wandering circus of new standard car models, also featuring dream cars. In 1952, the over 11,000 sports cars imported from Europe were indeed true dream cars. And GM had to keep up with the pace. GM's guests paid scant attention to President Eisenhower's inauguration on January 23, 1953. They were busily admiring the brand-new Chevrolet Corvette at the Waldorf-Astoria Hotel in New York.

In contrast to the mass-produced series, which simply slipped into a new outfit every year, the Corvette presented itself with near-European panache. The well-proportioned, smooth open-top body proclaimed itself as uncompromisingly sporty. Hence the symbolic emblem on the hood: chequered flag and Chevrolet flag. The headlights were protected from stones by a wire mesh; the armrests of the seats were cut individually from the body. A deeply mounted rear engine created a narrow overhang at the front, a low hood and lower centre of gravity, excellent for racing. On the other hand, the strongly drawn grille in the clear oval of the vent was reminiscent of the conservative Chevy sedan series.

Others would follow much later, but the Corvette had it in 1953: the panoramic windscreen with inverted A-column, modelled directly on the 1951 Buick show car, the Le Sabre. In other cars, the muffler pipe terminated gracelessly at the tail, but in the Corvette it was surrounded by chrome and positioned just below the left and right rear mudguards. These ended in round rear lights above which the tail fins mutated into two tiny fin stubs. The licence plate behind the flush rear window marked the middle. The technical basis was simple: the engine, called "Blue Flame," a synonym for the colour of the hottest-burning gas used in jet planes, had little real power with only six cylinders. The gears were standard, but the body was something completely new. It was fabricated in synthetic material thanks to the modest number of pieces—despite all the excitement, only 300 cars in 1953, but 3,640 cars in 1954. The dashboards of the mass-produced series were assembled from two segments, not unlike the shape of a cake-slice, one each in front of the driver and passenger, the former holding the speedometer, the latter the radio.

In 1956, there were pointed oval hollows behind the front wheels set off in a different colour, a distinct characteristic of the make until 1962. The round rear lights disappeared to give more emphasis to the headlights. The Corvette was less overwhelming in size and sheer metal volume than its initially more successful competitor, the Ford Thunderbird. Instead, it remained with increasingly powerful engines until the early 1970s. Thus, the Corvette displayed a consistency of line, continuity and character which Opel borrowed for its GT series, from 1968 through 1973, in an era when the "Vette" appeared with its "coke-bottle line" and Ferrari rear. H.-U.v.M.

Streamlined side panels, round headlights and a fashionable two-toned colour, 1956.

Slanted headlights and an open top emphasize the "coke-bottle-line" of 1971.

When the roof gets in the way, it can be removed in two sections, as in this 1974 model.

Towards the end of the 1990s, the Corvette's design loses its characteristic edge.

BIC "CRYSTAL" BALLPOINT PEN

László and George Biró, two Hungarian brothers, devised and patented their version of the ballpoint pen which may be seen as the direct antecedent of the BIC™ "Crystal" pen which has worldwide daily sales of up to 15 million. Indeed, the word "biro" has itself become a worldwide generic term for ballpoint pens. However, there had been a considerable number of precedents to the Birós' design, the earliest of which had been patented in 1888 by J. J. Loud, an American inventor. Although he had devised a pen for marking rough surfaces, dispensing ink by means of a ball-bearing which rolled across the surface to be inscribed, he did not foresee its wider commercial potential.

The Biró brothers' patent marked the advent of the modern ballpoint, utilizing a quick-drying ink associated with newspaper printing. After emigrating to Argentina, they took out a fresh patent in 1943, the licensing rights to which were bought by the British government. The Royal Air Force needed a new type of pen which would not leak at high altitudes in fighter planes, as had been the case with conventional fountain pens. The brothers' concept also attracted the attention of the U. S. War Department in 1944. The commercial application of the Biró design commenced in 1945, when it began to be marketed in Buenos Aires by the Eterpen Company, soon taken over by the Eversharp Company which sold the product as the "Eversharp CA" (Capillary Action). In October 1945, a close imitation was marketed by the Reynolds International Pen Company—millions of which sold within months, despite the fact that it performed poorly. Similar pens were also marketed in Britain by the Miles-Martin Pen Company.

For a while, sales increased dramatically. However, since many of the pens were of poor quality there was a dramatic fall in profits in the later 1940s, despite heavy advertising and a hefty decrease in price. Consumer confidence began to return with the highly successful introduction of the "Jotter" in 1954, the Parker Pen Company's first ballpoint. It was not only very efficient, but came in a variety of point sizes.

However, it was through the endeavours of Marcel Bich that the production of cheap, simple and functionally designed ballpoint pens became very much a commonplace item. Having established a pen factory in Clichy, France in 1953, he introduced the first BIC biro the same year. Within ten years, BIC had captured a large share of the European market for ballpoint pens and, having bought out New York-based Waterman Pens in 1958, began to sell the disposable, see-through, Crystal stick-pen in the United States. The company also determined to change the consumer's perception of the product through a national television advertising campaign with the slogan: "Writes First Time, Every Time!—and for only 29 cents."

The BIC Company has dominated the world market for biros for many years and is now an international sponsor of sporting events, as well as the producer of an increasingly wide spectrum of products, from sailboards to shavers.   J.M.W.

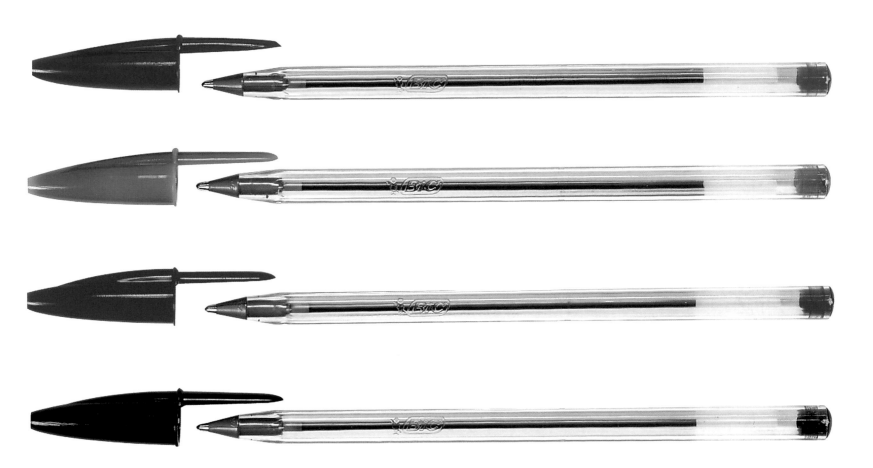

Inexpensive, simple and functional:
this disposable, see-through
pen quickly conquered the market.

ALU-CHAIR SERIES

Charles and Ray Eames

Charles and Ray Eames

Charles Eames was one of the most important, post-war, American furniture designers. Originally trained as an architect, he worked in close collaboration with his wife, Ray Eames (1913–1988). From 1941, their work as a partnership spanned film and exhibition design, toys, furniture, architecture and interior decoration. Charles Eames is famous for his quasi-sculptural approach to furniture design, expressed both in his prizewinning designs for ply-wood furniture and in his aluminium furniture, first produced by the Herman Miller Furniture Company in 1958.

Some furniture designers such as Marcel Breuer had already experimented with aluminium in the 1930s. An international competition for aluminium chairs had been held in Paris in 1933. And in 1938, Hans Coray (b. 1907) had designed the "Coray" aluminium chair, of which Eames had acquired an example in 1950. But these chairs were in the minority pre-war: aluminium was largely shunned for domestic furniture as being too expensive, inflexible and brittle. The Second World War transformed the aluminium industry, increasing produc-tion by 600 per cent. Post-1945, the American aluminium industry put a massive effort into promoting the use of the metal. The Eameses were among several designers commissioned by Alcoa to develop new products using the metal. Their aluminium chairs were first designed as outdoor furniture for the Irwin Miller home in Columbus, Indiana (1953–57; designed by Alexander Girard with the architect Eero Saarinen). The search was for something light and comfortable, which would also be resistant to corrosion.

Eames and his team developed an aluminium-framed chair with die-cast side panels and seating which was designed to resemble a hammock or swing. An "antler" joined the side pieces to the stem and base, while another acted as a brace on the rear of the seat frame. The sand-cast aluminium frame of the chair was technically challenging to produce, although the Eameses enjoyed its sculptural qualities. The "Sling" was gradually developed through several different experiments with materials. Initially, a fibrous plastic was used for the seating; later, this was replaced by a composite consisting of two layers of fabric and a vinyl filling, ultrasonically welded together. This was available in a variety of colours and offered comfort and durability.

The Alu-Chair was part of a series manufactured by the Herman Miller Furniture Company, which included large and small lounge chairs, a dining chair, an ottoman and dining and coffee tables with tops in slate, glass and Botticino marble. The smaller lounge chair originally sold for $168, with the larger model costing $252. They were never widely popular, on grounds of cost. However, they did have a certain appeal among artistic circles of the professional classes and were also taken up for executive use: with this end in view, two swivel chairs were added to the range in the 1960s. A further variant was introduced in 1969, with the creation of the "Soft Pad" group of chairs, which had separate cushions.   D.B.

The chairs of the Aluminium Group are available in many different models, from conference and office chairs on castors to comfortable armchairs for home.

GREYHOUND SCENICRUISER

Raymond Loewy

Raymond Loewy
Biography see p. 60

In October 1949, Raymond Loewy graced the front cover of *Time* magazine.

A native Parisian, Raymond Loewy emigrated to the United States in September 1919 to embark on a design career that would span almost 60 years. Between 1925 and 1980, Loewy almost single-handedly founded and exported the practice of industrial design—along with like-minded contemporaries Norman Bel Geddes, Henry Dreyfuss and Walter Dorwin Teague—via a network of international offices.

Early on, his impact on transportation—railroad, airline, automobile and bus industries—was profound: in 1939 he made an impression at the World's Fair in New York with his Railroad Service diorama and Chrysler Motors "Rocketport"—key exhibits in the fair's popular Transportation Zone—as well as his design of the official Greyhound intermural bus. In fact, it was not until Loewy's generation that designers had been called upon to shape the look of mass transit. It is to his credit that Loewy counted among his clients such giants of corporate America as the Pennsylvania Railroad, Lockheed, Boeing, Studebaker and Greyhound.

His relationship with the Greyhound Motorbus Company began in 1933 when Chief Executive Orville S. Caesar contracted him to refine the company's logo—in direct response to Loewy's comment that "the silhouette of the Greyhound ... on [their] buses ... suggested a fat mongrel" (Raymond Loewy, *Industrial Design*, 1979). Loewy's sleeker, leaner profile of the sprinting dog, combined with his later blue-and-white colour scheme, resulted in the more modern and streamlined look that remains a characteristic of the buses today.

Before the war, Greyhound also asked Loewy to develop a new bus that would seat a larger number of passengers. Already, he had been promoting a double-deck "Motorcoach of the Future," from which the Scenicruiser, built by General Motors, ultimately evolved. Work on the double-decker began in 1944, when Loewy rented a high-ceilinged, vacant store on the corner of Park Avenue and Forty-fifth Street in New York City in which to build a full-size mock-up of the bus, complete with seats and washroom. After extensive testing, the bus went into service in 1954 under the name Scenicruiser.

Unlike earlier double-deckers, characterized by stacked "slabs," Loewy's version was a long, sleek tube topped by a three-quarter-length observation deck. Inside was a spacious cabin with seats for 50 passengers—in contrast to earlier 37-seat models—whose upholstery was patterned in small, irregular shapes to disguise stains. For safety, Loewy reinforced the lower part of the bus at collision level and placed a large white disk with a dark red arrow on the inside of the door, pointing down towards the steps.

In response to the burgeoning post-war travel business and increasing competition from the railway and airline industries, Greyhound's Scenicruiser promoted the pleasures of the open highway via passenger amenities and high standards of safety. Nowadays, with airlines considered the first-class mode of "getting there," a long, interstate bus trip is hard to imagine. For its time, however, the Scenicruiser provided, on a mass scale, what the 1936 Airstream trailer afforded the individual: a moving panorama of the great American expanse viewed—through a picture window—from the distance and comfort of a self-contained environment.   C.S.

Elegant and comfortable, the double-deck Scenicruiser introduced a new era in long-distance bus travel.

In films and novels, the Greyhound symbolizes freedom and adventure in the vast expanse of America.

After Loewy updated their company logo, Greyhound's
"fat mongrel" metamorphosed into a trim greyhound.

ERICOFON

Hugo Blomberg

The original concept of the Ericofon was conceived in the early 1940s by a design team under the leadership of Hugo Blomberg at the Swedish telephone manufacturing company, Ericsson, in Stockholm. Their sophisticated, sculptural design was a reworking of the "candle-stick" or pedestal telephone often seen at the beginning of the twentieth century. It clearly distinguished itself from the vast majority of contemporary designs which generally followed the cradle and receiver type (often described in contemporary literature as a "cheese-dish") designed by Henry Dreyfuss for the Bell Telephone model manufactured by the Western Electric Company from 1950 onwards.

The Ericofon is clearly articulated, leaving the user no doubt about which parts are to be used for listening and speaking into, an attribute emphasized by the deep thumb-grip towards the base of the column. Furthermore, the basic notion was a simple one, resulting in the production of a compact instrument characterized by the elegant injection-moulded, thermoplastic casing which brought together the dialling mechanism, mouthpiece and earpiece in the "standset." Only the bellset and the capacitator were external elements. The rounded base rested on a pedestal of Neoprene rubber which lent the instrument sufficient grip on the work surface when not in use. The springset (which gives the dialling tone) took the form of a plastic button protruding slightly from the base which, when lifted, activated the dialling mechanism and which, when replaced on the work surface, deactivated it.

Despite the aura of apparent simplicity, this design solution took almost 15 years to refine, having seen a particular concentration of activity between 1949 and 1955. The design aim was to produce a modern telephone which was both light and easy to use, taking up a minimum of space on either a desk or table. The fresh possibilities afforded by miniaturization, which had evolved from developments in advanced electronic techniques, allowed the designer far greater freedom to concentrate on ergonomics and styling. In addition, there was a constant effort to reduce the weight and size of all components without compromising their technical performance. This resulted in a final product which weighed only 400 grams.

Described by the Swedish design journal *Form* as embodying the "art of our age," it was marketed in four pastel and two saturated colours in 1956. In 1957, *Design* magazine, published by the Council of Industrial Design in Britain, was slightly more circumspect in its evaluation of the success of the Ericofon. It commented that "the novelty of this idea has been widely recognised, but it will doubtless be tested in use for several years before the world passes judgement on its merit relative to more traditional designs." Although superseded by the mobile telephone revolution of recent years, the revolutionary Ericofon remained a design which could be found in fashionable, design-conscious retail outlets and museum collections of contemporary cultural icons for decades.   J.M.W.

Modern technology meets a new form: the Ericofon was a cut above other contemporary phone designs.

The first single-unit telephone in history, 1956.

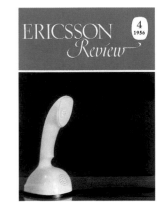

BRAUN PHONOSUPER SK4

Dieter Rams and Hans Gugelot

Dieter Rams

1932 Born on May 20 in Wiesbaden, Germany

1947–48 Studies architecture and interior architecture at the School for Applied Arts, Wiesbaden

1948–51 Apprentices as a trainee joiner in Kelkheim

1951–53 Continues his studies in Wiesbaden

1953–55 Employed by the Otto Appel architect's office in Frankfurt (which carries out joint projects with the American firm of Skidmore, Owings and Merrill)

1955–95 Employed as designer by Braun AG in Frankfurt and Kronberg (from 1961 onwards as chief designer); during this period he designs many products for Braun, including the Phonosuper SK4 (1956, in cooperation with Hans Gugelot), the Transistor 1 radio (1956), the T 1000 shortwave radio (1962), the TP1 portable radio-gramophone combination (1959), the ET44 pocket calculator (1978, in cooperation with Dietrich Lubs), the Cockpit 250 radio-gramophone combination (1970) and the Atelier hi-fi components (1980, in cooperation with Peter Hartwein)

1957 From now onwards designs furniture for Otto Zapf (now Wiese Vitsoe), Eschborn, including the "606" wall-furniture system (1960) and the "620" easy chair (1962)

1981 Appointed Professor at the Academy of Fine Arts, Hamburg

1987–97 President of the Rat für Formgebung (Committee for Form)

1999 Lives in Kronberg, Germany

Hans Gugelot
Biography see p. 129

There is a certain irony in the fact that a collaborative design by Dieter Rams and Hans Gugelot, of all people—perhaps the most renowned protagonists of "less is more"—should enter the annals of design history under the sentimental nickname "Schneewittchensarg" (Snow White's Coffin). Yet this nickname reveals an alternative interpretation which—quite apart from the trivializing and, incidentally, "in-house" parody—tells the success story behind this combination record player and wireless system. For this system did indeed lay something to rest in a coffin: the entire decorative pomposity of stereo equipment, cultivated so persistently in the early decades of the twentieth century until the founding years of the Federal Republic of Germany.

On the other hand, the Phonosuper SK4—a white metal sheet curved into a U-shape with wood panels attached at its sides and a Plexiglass cover—had none of the baroque weightiness of the *Volksempfänger* (People's Radio, see p. 56) and record-player cabinets which used to dominate German homes like altars. This piece of equipment was just that, a piece of equipment. No trace of furniture-like cladding concealed its technical purpose. On the contrary: the controls were arranged in an open yet austerely ordered manner, demonstrating operability.

But the SK4, a radio-gramophone combination, marked a turning point that went beyond form. Henceforth, radio and sound equipment ceased to be viewed as impressive showpieces but rather were seen as a combined compact system, a concept which had already been conceived in the 1920s and early 1930s. Further, the ability to combine the individual components was no longer considered solely from the aspect of fixed assembly, rather it included the option of loose assembly, which opened the door to developing a system.

This system concept was hinted at in the first sets developed by Gugelot for Braun between 1955 and 1956. The dimensions of the G-12 record player, for example, were such that, in combination with the G-11-Super radio receiver, they would match the exact height of the FS-G television set, which was designed and developed at the same time. The so-called hi-fi system was born. It has become a standard feature in our homes whose typology remains virtually unchanged.

V.A.

The transparent cover made an international impact and gained the model the nickname Snow White's Coffin.

The uncompromising shape of the radio-gramophone SK4 hints at the straight lines of 1960s design.

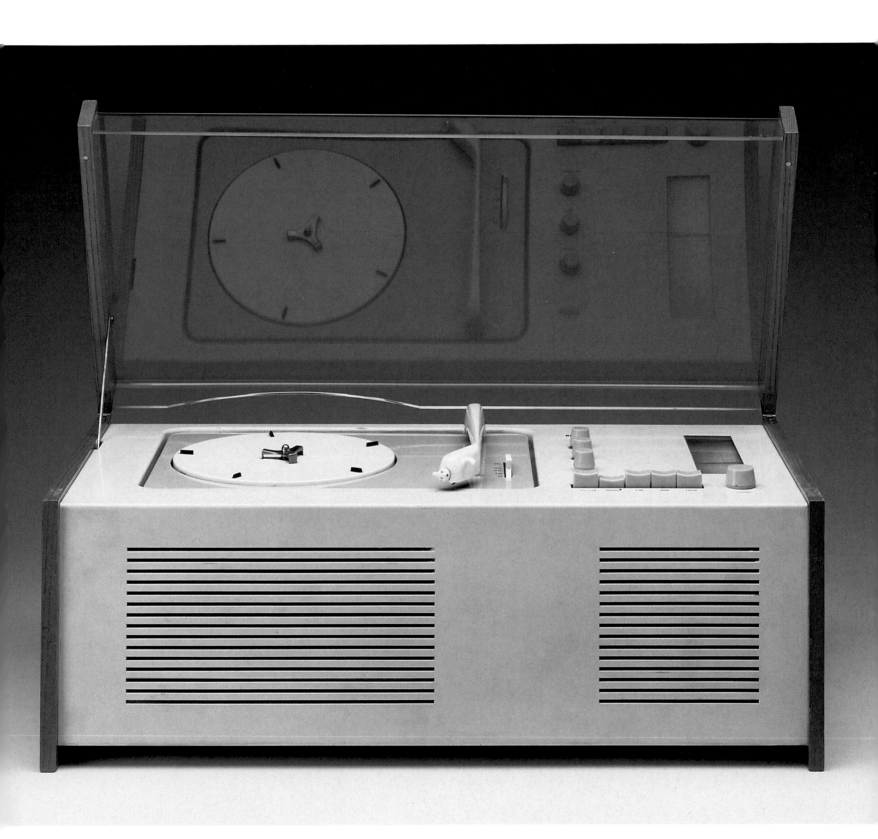

LEGO

Ole Kirk and Godtfred Christiansen

During the world economic crisis in the 1930s, Danish cabinet-maker Ole Kirk Christiansen made wooden toys for local farmers, and, after 1934, he called his small company LEGO, a composite of the first syllables of the Danish words *leg* (to play) and *godt* (good). In 1947, he purchased the first injection-moulding machine in all of Denmark to cast pre-notched building blocks. But it was his son, Godtfred, who invented the actual notch principle and patented it. From that point forward, success took off. Since the notched building blocks were introduced to the market some 70 years ago, Lego has grown from a small family operation to Europe's largest toy manufacturer. Founded in Denmark, Scandinavia's smallest nation, the company continues to maintain its seat in the village of Billund. But today, the small community boasts the country's second largest airport, thanks to financial support from the manufacturer, as well as Legoland, which features 50 replicas of towns from 7 countries of northern Europe—realistically reconstructed in Lego blocks. In addition to the classic blocks in the primary colours and black and white, there are large blocks for pre-schoolers and, more recently, some 20 individual product lines for special target groups such as romantic teenagers or technology crazed boys. New interactive computer blocks are giving learning computers, video games and Gameboys a run for their money in children's playrooms everywhere. Merchandising and licenced products, for example in the clothing sector, are yet another indicator of the label's popularity: it has become one of the most successful designer ideas of the century, as familiar as Coca Cola, McDonald's or Volkswagen. Since their invention, approximately 190 billion pieces have been sold; statistically, therefore, each person worldwide owns approximately 30 notched blocks. There is probably no other toy that rivals Lego blocks in terms of fame. According to estimates, some 300 million children and adults throughout the world have become hobby building masters thanks to this fabulous toy idea.

Plastic for child's play—Lego's notched building blocks are popular with children around the world.

Educators, as well as the company itself, have recognized and praised the socializing and communication-enhancing potential of the toy, the "effective, three-dimensional modelling aid" for the young person's perception and comprehension of the world. The structure of the blocks follows a strict logic and thus promotes compatible, methodical thinking. Some ten years ago, the German designer and design philosopher Otl Aichler observed that: "To grasp something in your mind is more than a mere visual analogy to [the] physical [act of] grasping. A culture of the mind cannot exist without a true culture of the hand. ...If the hand is allowed to reach its full potential, if it does more than just work but also plays ...then the mind will develop more freely too. Plasticity in the hand is plasticity in the mind, the object grasped is the idea grasped."   V.F.

When Barbie made her debut at the 1959 American Toy Fair, wearing nothing but a black-and-white bathing suit, no one imagined that she would become the world's most famous doll as well as a cult object and collectors' item. Ostracized by many parents, feminists and pedagogues, the unwavering appeal of this miniature mannequin with impossible anatomic proportions is a marketing phenomenon: more than 1 billion Barbie dolls have been sold in some 140 countries around the world, and in Europe and the United States more than 90 per cent of girls between the ages of 3 and 10 own at least one Barbie doll.

Barbie is considered the all-American girl but, in fact, her roots are German. The sassy, blond "Lilli" doll, based on a comic strip figure in the newspaper *Bild*, appeared on the German market in 1955, targeted at an adult audience. Three years later, Ruth Handler, co-founder of the American toy company, Mattel, discovered Lilli while travelling in Europe. She was convinced that an adult-figured doll for children would fill a gap in a market dominated by baby dolls. Mattel bought the rights for Lilli, and the remarkably similar-looking Barbie doll—named after Handler's daughter—was introduced to the American market as a "teen-age fashion model—a new kind of doll from real life." Buyers initially gave Barbie a cool reception, considering her explicit female curves unmarketable. After all, if Barbie was life-sized, her hourglass measurements would equal 39–18–33 inches. But children proved the experts wrong: advertised as a glamorous but affordable fashion doll, more than 350,000 were sold within a year.

The original, or No. 1, Barbie was 11½ inches tall, wore her hair in a ponytail with straight fringe, had red lips and nails and heavy black eyeliner. Though the pedestal that the first dolls came with was soon abandoned, Mattel never changed Barbie's basic physique but continued carefully to alter details to tailor her to the fashions of the day and keep her competitive. Early on, she smelled like crayon, while the colour of her skin faded to a ghostly ivory and her ears turned green as a reaction to her pearl earrings. Those teething troubles were overcome quickly, though, and countless enhancements of Barbie's bodily movements and facial expressions made her ever more realistic. When multicultural appeal became crucial in an increasingly global market, the blond, blue-eyed prototype was joined over the years by African-American, Asian and Hispanic Barbies.

The secret of Barbie's success is that she was created without a fixed personality. She should be whoever her owner wanted her to be, and through a multitude of ensembles and accessories she could be transformed into almost every role. Handler recognized that "the doll sells fashion and fashion sells the doll," and so Barbie's huge wardrobe has always been as important as the doll itself. Borrowing from haute couture and ready-to-wear at the same time, but always with meticulous attention to details, such as miniature zippers and buttons, Mattel's designers made sure that Barbie followed every decade's major fashion trends, from petticoats to bell-bottoms, disco glitter to baggy pants. Even some of the greatest designers, including Christian Dior and Calvin Klein, have created outfits for her. And just beyond 40, Barbie is still looking pretty good.   C.H.

Pretty in pink: primping for an important date!

(from top to bottom)
A creation by the American fashion designer, Bob Mackie.

Leather fringe, batik patterns and bell-bottom pants (1971): Barbie follows every fashion trend.

In 1980, the first black Barbie was introduced on the market.

"Enchanted Evening":
gown with fur stole, 1960–63.

Barbie No. 1 (left)
was the first doll.

The introduction of the Mini Cooper drastically increased sales figures in the 1960s.

Mary Quant's boutique: the Mini car meets the maker of the miniskirt.

The Morris Mini evolved out of a corporate desire to create a small, affordable, economic urban vehicle. The petrol rationing which followed the Suez Crisis of 1956 inspired Sir Leonard Lord, President of the British Motor Corporation, to commission the project from the company's chief engineer, Alec Issigonis. The plan was to produce a design which was 3.04 metres in length, from bumper to bumper, with 80 per cent of the car's space devoted to the passengers and their baggage. This necessitated considerable ingenuity, including a transverse 848-cubic-centimetre engine to power the front wheels—themselves only about 25 centimetres in diameter with special tyres commissioned from Dunlop—and a compressed rubber suspension system. It was a remarkably effective solution, and its quintessential practicality embodied Issigonis' maxim that "styling is for obsolescence." Like Giacosa in respect of the Topolino (see p. 72), Issigonis worked with a select group of specialists who helped bring his radical ideas to fruition.

Remarkably, following a frenetic period of research, development and preparation for production, the car was launched as the Morris Mini and Austin 7 in 1959, only two years after its conception. But despite considerable publicity and a price of £497 for the standard model, the Mini failed to attract large numbers of buyers in its first year of manufacture. However, with the introduction of the Mini Cooper in 1961 and its subsequent success on the rally circuit—including victories at the Monte Carlo rallies of 1964 and 1965—its sales reached a million by 1965. It also became closely identified with notions of urban chic and the London of the celebrated "Swinging Sixties," even if sales analyses revealed it to be owned by a far wider social spectrum. Over 40 years later, it remains a visible part of British urban culture.

J.M.W.

Alec Issigonis

1906	Born on November 18 in Smyrna (now Izmir), Turkey
1923–27	Studies mechanical engineering at Battersea Polytechnic, London
1928–32	Works in Edward Gillet's design office in London
1933–36	Works as a technical draughtsman for the car manufacturer Humber in Coventry
1936	Joins Morris Motors in Cowley, where he designs suspension systems for cars, including the 1939 series "M Morris Ten"
1939	Designs and builds his own racing car, the Lightweight Special
1947–48	Morris Minor car
1952–55	Works for the Alvis Car Company, Coventry
1956	Returns to Morris (now merged with Austin)
1957–59	Morris Mini Minor car (also sold under the name Austin Seven)
1962–69	Designs more cars for Morris: Austin-Morris 1100 (1962), Austin-Morris 1800 (1964–65), Austin-Morris Maxi (1968–69)
1972–88	After his retirement, acts as a design consultant to the British Motor Corporation and to British-Leyland (successors to Austin-Morris)
1988	Dies on October 2 in Birmingham

Still swinging in London: the Mini is a permanent fixture in British urban culture.

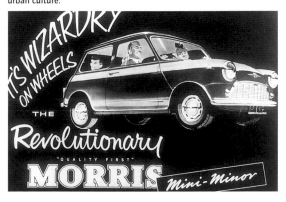

SONY PORTABLE TV 80 301

Sony Design Centre

The Sony Company, founded in 1946 by businessman Akio Morita, belongs to the leading manufacturers of consumer electronics worldwide. Originally called Tokyo Tsushin Kogye Kabushikakaika, the company name was changed to Sony in 1958. The word not only reminds one of the Latin word *sonus* for "sound," but is also understood in Japan as the diminutive form of the English word "son." This "little son" developed quickly into an internationally active, globally operative firm. In contrast to Western custom, Japanese companies employ permanent design teams who normally remain anonymous. During Japan's reconstruction phase after the Second World War, Sony produced the first tape recorder, bought the manufacturing rights to the transistor—an American discovery—and, building on these, released the first transistor radio onto the market in 1955. In 1959, the first portable, battery-operated, transistor television set of its kind followed. Boasting a 46-centimetre screen and a solid handle for carrying, the TV 80 301 weighed a mere 6 kilograms. The channel and volume dials are found on top of the rounded metal casing, the telescope antenna is on the back and the on/off switch is beneath the slightly convex television screen. A movable filter, adjustable by means of knurled screws, protects the screen like sunglasses from strong light and glare. The general trend of the time period was to design an aesthetically appealing product, one that set it apart from the others. This, however, was not crucial to the success of the 80 301 television. Its size and superior technology left it without competitors, and this approach became the nucleus of Sony's entire product development and sales strategy.

Later, too, Sony brought other innovations onto the market, thereby expanding the history of this chapter in consumer electronics: the company produced the first home video recorder in 1964, the professional U-matic video format in 1969 and the first Walkman in 1979 (see p. 146), followed by hundreds of variations not only from Sony but from all corresponding manufacturers. The same happened with the Discman, which was ready for the market in 1980. Its technological prerequisite, the discovery of the digital CD (see p. 148), was a collaborative project between Sony and Philips. Yet, among thousands of different products that have since been produced, Sony—like many Japanese manufacturers—generally followed the strategy into the 1980s of creating new products from existing ones.   V.F.

In 1960, Sony's technical innovation was awarded the gold medal at the Milan Triennale.

PANTON SIDE CHAIR

Verner Panton

Verner Panton

The Danish architect and designer, Verner Panton, was one of the foremost designers in plastics. In 1955, Panton, while working for Arne Jacobsen (1902–1971) in Copenhagen, designed the first, all-plastic, stackable chair without legs. This ingenious chair, made in one piece and manufactured by injection-moulding technique from 1960 until 1967 by the Herman Miller Company in Switzerland, was originally made with fiberglass-reinforced polyester. Upon removing the chair from its formwork, burrs on all the edges had to be laboriously sanded away by hand. After the switch to polyurethane hard foam, this became easier. In 1990, following renewed interest in classic, plastic designs of the 1960s, Vitra acquired the rights to reissue the chair as the "Panton" chair.

In contrast to other plastic chairs of its time—such as those by Joe Colombo (1930–1971), Eliel Saarinen (1873–1951), Vico Magistretti (b. 1920) or Helmut Bätzner—Panton replaced the four legs—the trumpet foot, or, as the case may be, the double U-profile of the tubular-steel chair—with the open half of a dynamically bowed cone, to which the concave shell of the seat and back surface organically connect. The curved S-form, only statically possible in this manner and seen in the chair's side elevation, expressed to a "T"—or rather, in this case, an "S"—the optimism of Pop Art sculpture of this era, with its graphic, colourful and plastic appearance. Editions from the 1960s, in orange-red or off-white, are still on the market today and frequently offered by international auction houses. With more than a quarter million copies sold, this chair clearly represents Panton's most successful design and is an icon within the euphoria over plastics. During Panton's lifetime, he helped this material to find its appropriate expression in the form of numerous lamps, seats and chairs—among others the ice-cream-cone-shaped "Heart," "Cone" and "Wire Cone" chairs of the late 1950s—and above all, in the "Visiona 2" foam landscape with its psychedelic colour patterns at the 1970 International Furniture Fair in Cologne. V.F.

The plastic, sculptural chair was a sensation in the 1960s and gained numerous prizes. One of the earliest models is in the Museum of Modern Art, New York.

In recent years, progress in plastics processing has resulted in yet another development of the chair without legs. The latest version of the Panton chair is made of polypropylene and was created in close cooperation with Verner Panton.

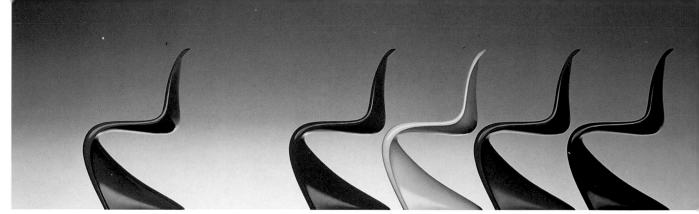

IBM SELECTRIC TYPEWRITER

Eliot Noyes

This design, in many ways an aesthetic embodiment of Eliot Noyes's corporate design philosophy at IBM, represented a technological shift through its incorporation of a distinctive feature. This was a spherical, single-element mechanism (popularly known as a "golfball") that replaced the conventional arrangement of individual type-bars which printed characters onto paper positioned in a moving carriage. In fact, the golfball, which contained 88 characters, moved along the page with the typing whilst the carriage remained static. However, this concept dated back to the early years of the typewriter, the 1880s, when several manufacturers had introduced single-element mechanisms into their machines. In fact, the conceptual resemblance to the Selectric did not end there: the Blick Electric typewriter of 1902 was both powered by electricity and incorporated the single element. Just as the Underwood Typewriter No. 5 of 1900 (see p. 15) had incorporated ideas from earlier models and set a standard to which rival manufacturers aspired, so it was with the IBM Selectric. The latter's aesthetic clarity was not seriously challenged until the arrival of the first electronic typewriter, the Exxon QYX in 1978, which incorporated a microprocessor and "daisy wheel" typing mechanism.

The clean, modernist aesthetic, or International Style, which characterized much of Noyes's work, was perhaps enhanced through contact with Marcel Breuer and Walter Gropius while working in their office in Cambridge, Massachussetts (1938–40). His commitment to such an outlook was further consolidated through his time in charge of the Department of Industrial Design at the Museum of Modern Art in New York (1940–42), where many leading European modernists and their work had been exhibited during the previous decade. He became design consultant to IBM in 1956, when he began to bring in leading designers and architects for the creation of a clearly articulated corporate identity. The elegance of the Selectric and other well-designed office equipment of the 1950s and 1960s helped to endow office work with a sense of status, clearly removed from often lucrative but unappealing work on the factory floor. Indeed, the Selectric has been likened by one writer to "desk-top sculpture." J.M.W.

Eliot Noyes

1910   Born in Boston, Massachusetts
1935   Architectural degree from the Harvard Graduate School of Design, Massachusetts
1938   Works for Walter Gropius and Marcel Breuer, Cambridge, Massachusetts
1940   First director of industrial design for the Museum of Modern Art, New York (until 1942 and then 1945–46)
1946   Works in the office of Norman Bel Geddes
1947   Has his own design office in New Canaan, Connecticut; works for Westinghouse, Mobil Oil Company, Pan American World Airways and Xerox
1947–56 Art and design critic for the *Consumer Report*
1954   Award for his house in New Canaan
1956   Begins design work for IBM; responsible for corporate identity
1965–70 President of the International Design Conference, Aspen, Colorado
1977   Dies in New Canaan

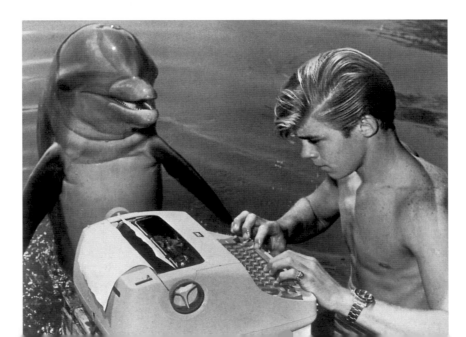

Only the best technology for Flipper's secretary: in the 1960s, IBM used Hollywood's popular dolphin in its advertisements.

The Selectric's spherical head or "golfball" was innovative because it was removable.

The SM-3 electric razor was introduced on the market in 1960. While its shape was quite similar to the Sixtant, it was not as technically sophisticated.

Every sector of product design, whether appliance, furniture or automotive, contains outstanding examples that remain models for years, if not decades, for all other variations. For electric razors, this has been the uncontested privilege of the Braun Sixtant designed by Gerd Alfred Müller and Hans Gugelot in 1961 and introduced on the market in 1962.

Even today, ask any child to draw an electric razor and most will sketch an image that has some resemblance to this Braun model: an upright that curves gently outwards, or, to use an elegant contemporary expression, an exploded cuboid, almost evenly divided in a three-to-one ratio, black on the bottom and white, or silver, on top.

But what makes this design a model for others? What—apart from its innovation (spring-loaded razor, galvanoplastically formed six-edged blade)—is the mark of a product that sets the standard for all others? To begin with, there is the ergonomic quality. The measurements, overall volume and shape of the housing, are a perfect fit for the grip of a male hand. And the razor head, an expanded *U* in cross section, is indeed ideal in form.

Yet, these purely haptic characteristics are only partially responsible for the success of the Braun Sixtant. The design itself has contributed at least to equal measure. For while the white used for its predecessor, the SM-3, also designed by Müller, still subscribed to the colour code that was traditional for all personal hygiene utensils, the black colour catapulted the razor onto a different plane altogether. Moreover, thanks to the vertically grooved matte finish of the plain, plastic housing and the chrome steel, humble materials acquired an aura of luxury that had been completely lacking in the image of previous models.

With the Sixtant, Braun created a status symbol for modern men. The design of the Braun Sixtant, especially the combination of black and silver, set the trend for decades to come, not just for Braun products but for all household and electronic appliances. Even today, this colour and material combination is synonymous with understated and timeless design.

V.A.

Hans Gugelot

1920   Born on April 1 in Makassar, Celebes (Indonesia), as a Dutch citizen

1940   Studies at the Engineering School, Lausanne and at the Technical University, Zurich

1945–46 Degree in architecture

1948–50 Works for Max Bill; first furniture designs

1950   Has his own office; development of the "M-125" modular furniture system

1954   Teaches at the School for Design, Ulm, Germany; first contact with Erwin Braun

1955   Design teacher (and later head) of the Development Group II at the School for Design, Ulm; develops the new Braun appliance design, presented at the German Radio and Television Exhibition, Düsseldorf

1956   Improves construction of the M-125 furniture system; mass-produced by Wilhelm Bofinger

1957   Grand prize at the eleventh Milan Triennale for the Braun product line

1962   Founds the Institut für Produktionsent-wicklung und Design e. v. (Institute for product development and design) in Neu-Ulm (succeeded in 1966 by Gugelot Design Gmbh, founded by Malke Gugelot

1964   Begins development of the first sports car with self-supporting floor structure in plastic

1965   Dies on October 9 in Ulm, Germany

Gerd Alfred Müller

1932   Born on August 24 in Frankfurt, Germany

1952–55 Studies interior design at the School of Crafts and Design, Wiesbaden

1955–60 Full-time professional capacity at Braun in Frankfurt, where he designs some of his best-known products, above all kitchen appliances and razors

1956   Collaborates with Dieter Rams and the model builder Roland Weigend at Braun

1960   Founds an industrial and graphic design studio in Eschborn; designs for the Heidelberg pen manufacturer Lamy, e. g. "Lamy 2000" (1966) and "Lamy Twin" (1984)

1991   Dies on December 6 in Eschborn, Germany

The Braun Sixtant was not just the top of the line in terms of make but the epitome of style in its day.

ARCO LAMP
Achille Castiglioni

The Arco lamp has an arch which can reach into space nearly 2 metres, while its heavy marble base provides a sturdy counterweight.

Achille Castiglioni

1918	Born on February 16 in Milan as the son of the sculptor and painter Giannino Castiglioni
1944	Completes architectural studies at the Milan Politecnico
1945	Design office together with his brothers Pier Giacomo and Livio Giacomo (who leaves the office in 1952)
1947	Begins to participate in all Milan Triennales; wins the Compasso d'Oro nine times
1956	Co-founder of the Associazione per il Disegno Industriale, A.D.I. (Association for Industrial Design)
1970–77	Teaches interior design and furniture design at the Turin Politecnico
1981–86	Professor of interior design and furniture design at the Milan Politecnico
1986	Begins professorship in industrial design at the Milan Politecnico; honorary member of the department of industrial design at the Royal Society of Art, London

Castiglioni's Arco floor lamp is one of the pre-eminent icons of Italy's post-war, Italian design movement. Designed in 1962 and manufactured by Flos at the peak of that movement's influence, it denotes the level of aesthetic sophistication that characterizes that country's contribution to post-war design.

The lamp's main structural element consists of a stainless-steel arch made up of four pieces of curved tubing which fit together telescopically. The thickest element is fixed into a marble base, the weight of which ensures that the light remains firmly on the floor in spite of the wide span of the steel arch. The heavy marble block has a hole pierced through it, enabling the user to move the light into the required position. Attached to the thinnest element of the arch, which finishes in mid-air rather than returning to the floor, is the light source contained within a rounded reflector made of polished aluminium. The top of the reflector is pierced by a number of holes which allow the light to emanate from the top of it as well as from the bottom. The arch is 244 centimetres at its highest point, and it reaches 188 centimetres into the space in which it is situated.

The Arco lamp is a prominent object that is hard to ignore. In the 1960s, it could be found in many fashionable interiors, whether hovering over a desk as a task light, over a dining table to enhance a meal, over a sofa as a reading light or as a means of illuminating objects displayed on a coffee table. Through the 1950s and 1960s, Italy used the lighting object as a symbol of its modernization programme, of the shift from the dark interiors of traditional rural dwellings to the bright spaces within cosmopolitan, urban interiors. Lighting design also offered a perfect sculptural opportunity for designers, since it brought art together with utility.

Castiglioni's choice of modern materials made it the perfect accompaniment for leather sofas and smoked-glass tables. At the same time, the links between the traditional material, marble, and Italy's heroic past were also significant, as the modern Italian design movement had a strong nationalist agenda. On one level, Arco represented a sense of continuity between past and present. Visually, it acted as a strong punctuation mark in modern Italian interiors, confirming their claim to be "of their age." The lamp was widely featured on the covers of glossy interior design magazines throughout the 1960s and 1970s, and was a familiar appendage in the stylish interiors depicted in numerous Italian "B" movies from the period. It suggested a level of confidence, opulence and stylishness which has never been repeated in Italy's history nor in the story of post-war design in general.

Within Castiglioni's oeuvre, the Arco lamp holds a special place. It marks the peak of his professional career, which began in the immediate post-war years, when, with his older brother Pier Giacomo (1913–1968), he designed a wide range of exhibition displays, interiors and products which have had a lasting impact.   P.S.

SAMSONITE ATTACHÉ CASE

The Samsonite attaché case, first launched in 1962, heralded a revolution in the design of executive luggage. The rapid increase in worldwide air travel brought about a demand for luggage which was tough, smart and durable. Leather briefcases and attaché cases were challenged first by fiberglass and then by polypropylene, hard-shell attaché cases. The American luggage manufacturer, Samsonite, played a key role in this revolution.

Samsonite cases were—and are—extremely tough and scratch-resistant, thus highly suited for the rapid evolution of executive air travel. Their clean, streamlined appearance with recessed lock plates and moulded handles fit the style of the modern jet-setting businessman. The classic attaché case became the first Samsonite product to be thoroughly researched before it was launched. This, together with a national advertising campaign, paved the way for its commercial success.

Samsonite is now a worldwide luggage group. It started in the United States at the beginning of the twentieth century. Jesse Shwayder, a Polish immigrant businessman from Denver, Colorado went into the luggage business, first retail and then manufacturing. He proved to have a genius for marketing. Starting in 1908, with $3,500 in borrowed capital and a small factory in Denver, he and his family established the Shwayder Trunk Manufacturing Co.. By 1923, annual sales had soared to $690,000. Shwayder favoured the trade name "Samsonite" because of its biblical associations with strength. He advertised the durability and strength of his products dramatically, showing one of his cases supporting a plank of wood on which he, his father and three brothers stood. Today, as then, the company's products are noted for their strength, durability, quality and style and also for the wit and impact of their advertisements. The business expanded to Detroit, as other products were introduced. These included groups of coordinating luggage—manufactured in vulcanized fiberboard and finished to resemble leather—as well as folding tables and chairs.

The first executive attaché cases were introduced in 1958, using fiberglass for their shell construction. The search for new materials led to the introduction of polyvinyl chloride, which could be injection-moulded, creating products with a uniform colour and texture. The attaché case was such a runaway success that, in 1966, Samsonite introduced a second, mid-priced version to satisfy demand. A subsidiary company was established in Australia, manufacturing attaché cases under licence. The principles embodied in the design and manufacture of the classic attaché case were developed further in 1969, with the launch of the "Saturn," the first polypropylene suitcase whose structure was fully supported by injection-moulded shells.

Today, the group manufactures stylish and durable hard-shell suitcases, alongside fashionable, soft-side luggage. It is now a multinational group, with European headquarters in Belgium and subsidiaries in India and China linked to its U.S. parent.   D.B.

Regardless of its contents, the Samsonite attaché case gives its owner a professional look.

The Shwayder family demonstrate the strength and durability of a Samsonite attaché case.

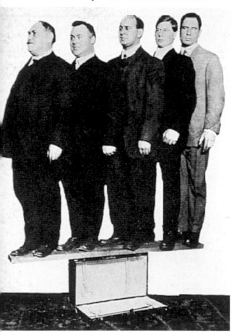

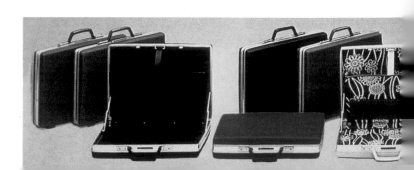

SEX ⚥ SHOP

FILMS ★ BOOKS ★ BIZARRE ★ LINGERIE ★ MAGAZIENS ★

Peu importe ce que contient votre attaché case Samsonite, vous avez toujours l'air aussi sérieux.

Avec un attaché case Samsonite, vous avez toujours l'air de quelqu'un de sérieux. La sobriété de ses formes, la solidité de sa construction ont quelque chose d'anglo-saxon qui vous pose un homme. Et surtout les attaché cases Samsonite sont d'une remarquable discrétion.

Noir, gris ou brun, ils possèdent tous une serrure inviolable (parfois même à combinaison), un cadre qui résiste aux chocs et un aménagement intérieur qui permet un rangement efficace.

Pourtant le sérieux n'exclut pas la variété. Classic 100, Classic IV, Signat II, nos attaché cases existent en plusieurs tailles. Et pour moins cher qu'on ne croit: ils coûtent de 245 F à 475 F.

Alors n'attendez plus. Un attaché case Samsonite, c'est la manière la plus élégante de ne pas se faire remarquer.

TBWA

Samsonite S.A.R.L., 112-120, rue Vaillant Couturier, 93 Noisy-le-Sec

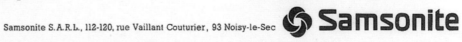 ❖ Samsonite

BRIONVEGA RADIO TS-502

Marco Zanuso and Richard Sapper

Marco Zanuso

1916	Born on May 14 in Milan
1935–39	Architectural studies at the Milan Politecnico
1945	Begins work as a self-employed architect
1947–49	Publisher of the magazine *Casabella*; works for the magazine *Domus*
1948	Commissioned by Pirelli to experiment with a new material, latex foam; "Antropus" chair, 1949
1951	Founds the firm Arflex for the serial production of plastic foam chairs; receives gold medal for the "Lady" chair and grand prize at the Milan Triennale for the "Triennale" sofa, from which Zanuso developed the "Sleep-O-Matic" sofa bed in 1954
1955–57	Architect for Olivetti in São Paulo and Buenos Aires
1957–59	President of the Associazione per il Disegno Industriale (A.D.I.)
1958	Exhibition spaces for the Necchi company, Pavia
1960–63	Exhibition spaces for the Feal company, Milan
1961–77	Collaboration with Richard Sapper
1961–64	Children's chair in injected polyethylene for the firm of Kartell (the first large object in non-reinforced plastic)
1964	In collaboration with Sapper, designs the "Lambda" chair from one piece of coated sheet metal
1966–74	President of the A.D.I.
1970	Exhibition spaces for Edgars Limited, Johannesburg
1976	Appointed professor at the Milan Politecnico

Richard Sapper
Biography see p. 144

Among the many icons that Italy produced in the 1960s, Zanuso and Sapper's little TS-502 radio of 1964 has a special place. Both designers had worked as consultants to the electronics manufacturing company, Brionvega, for half a decade by that time, and had previously produced a radically different television set for them (the Doney 14) before the radio appeared. They went on through the 1960s to produce other seminal television sets—the Algol of 1964 and the Black 201, the ultimate black box in 1969. For an entire decade, therefore, they focused on designing advanced electronics in which both function and looks were "state of the art."

This was a particularly Italian project. While Japan looked to technological novelty, and Germany to rational design which emphasized function, Italy sought a design solution which would combine art and technology in a new formula. The TS-502 was a classic result of this Italian preoccupation. When closed, it was a small enigmatic box with no excrescences—the chrome handle and aerial folded into the surface to create a flush finish. The black, white, orange and yellow monoliths thus created were small "Pop" sculptures which existed in their own right as material forms to be reckoned with. When opened, however, the function of the object was quickly revealed. While one half housed the loudspeaker, the other contained the controls. The latter were arranged in two, neat semicircles with a row of knobs carefully positioned within them. The composition of the elements on the control panel was a highly sophisticated graphic exercise. The interior was essentially black with red-and-white details highlighted against the dark backdrop. Separating the exterior from the interior were bright chrome strips which demarcated form from function when open and which blended together when the object reverted to being pure form.

The TS-502 is strongly controlled down to every last detail. Its form is its meaning, and the separation of sculptural object from utility item within a single form is semantical as well as literal. It is a highly sophisticated object in design terms, far ahead of its time. Stylistically, it belonged to the same world as the brightly coloured plastic chairs designed by Zanuso and Sapper, Vico Magistretti (b. 1920), Joe Colombo (1930–1971) and others—icons of an age which still fetishized technology and believed in the future. The notion of the synthetic was still a vital one, and new materials still represented a powerful means of moving forward. In the TS-502, Zanuso and Sapper expressed all of these themes within a single object.   P.S.

The portable TS-502 radio cleverly closes to form a solid rectangular cube.

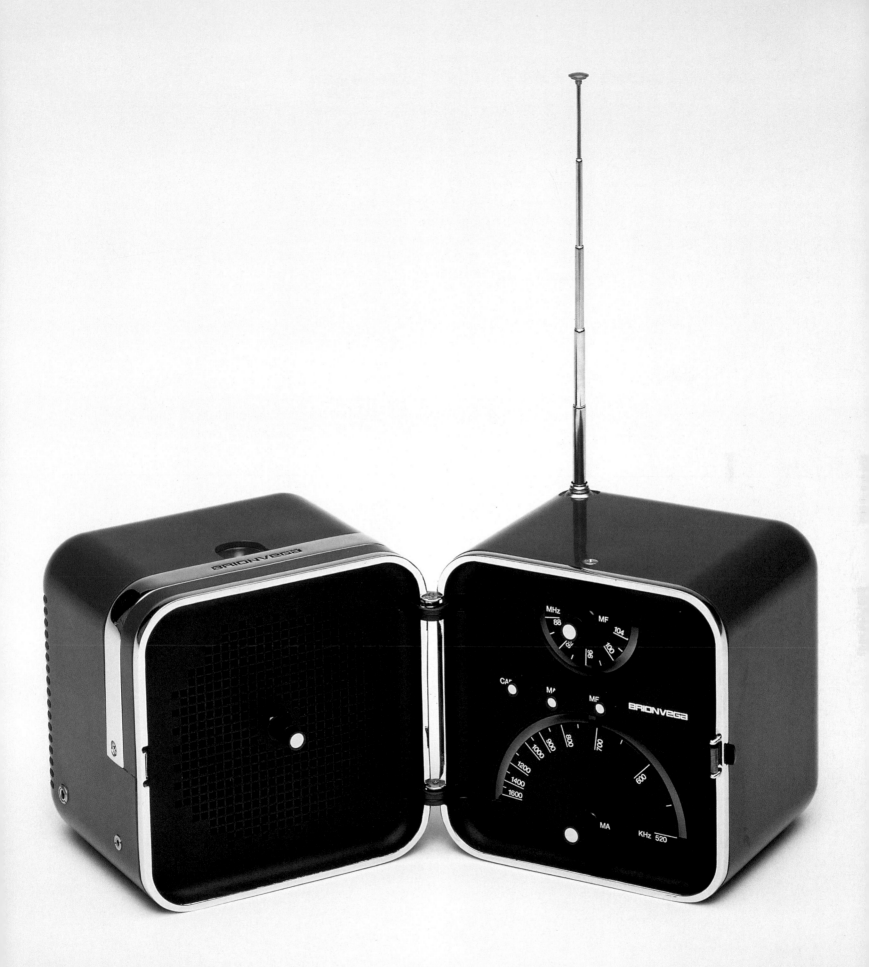

HARLEY DAVIDSON "EASY RIDER" CHOPPER

Film stills from *Easy Rider* (1969)
with Dennis Hopper and Peter Fonda.

Among a select few design objects, the Harley Davidson motorbike exists as an international icon, achieving a mythic status forged largely in Hollywood. Not a production model, this "Panhead" chopper from the 1969 movie *Easy Rider* is the most recognized motorcycle in the world, an archetype defining motorcycling to the non-riding public. Two of these bikes are supposed to have been made: one was destroyed on film and the other stolen before the movie's release. Reportedly none of the original bikes are still extant, although many replicas have since appeared. Peter Fonda, the star and producer of the movie, conceived the design using a tried-and-true formula and hired a customizer, Cliff Voss, to transform several surplus California Highway Patrol Harleys. Their custom features, loaded with cartoonish hyperbole and an almost obscene exhaust sound, telegraphed raw power; choppers both parodied authority and embodied the extravagance of post-war American culture. In addition to its primary function as transportation, the sheer excess of the chopped "Hog" was formulated to capture attention. From the start, riders have individualized their bikes, often radically altering the geometry of the machine as it was manufactured. Choppers were lightened and lengthened for straight-line performance, a less-is-more ethic demanded by drag racing. Often as the result of a crash, riders on a budget cut away nonessential damaged parts, such as fenders, and made do without them, or reconfigured their ride using junk (or stolen) parts.

Although motorcycles have always exuded danger, a series of sensational exposés and the 1954 movie, *The Wild One*, taught the public to distinguish outlaws from law-abiding motorcyclists by differentiating motorcycles by type. The Harley Chopper marked the rebel biker: an oil-stained, tattooed and chain-wielding hooligan who wore a black leather jacket emblazoned with the emblem of a motorcycle gang. As portrayed in the press and in legions of pulpy books and movies, bikers and chopped Harleys were understood to be a sad parable of the moral decline of America's youth. Crazed by drugs and alcohol, rumbling packs of mounted "Visigoths" descended upon lonely villages to carry away maidens—sometimes compliant—for their diabolical purposes.

Somewhat altering this archetype, *Easy Rider* portrayed the biker as a crusader for the mythic elixir of the American West, a visionary who rekindled America's pioneer spirit from its conformity within a status-seeking establishment. The chopper, thus, evokes several divergent myths: American technical ingenuity, the characters of the Wild West and the romantic revolutionary. As the Vietnam-era, with its counterculture image, faded into the economic malaise of the 1970s, Harleys became the symbol for patriotic tenacity, of embattled American manufacturers and workers. In the 1980s and 1990s, Harley Davidson pioneered retro-styling. This production correlated to the public's growing nostalgia for the heroic lifestyle presented in *Easy Rider*. These mass-produced, "custom" bikes represented a means of escape and self-realization for overworked and underinspired professionals.   R.S.

A 1993 replica of the legendary Harley Davidson *Easy Rider* Chopper of 1969.

PLIA FOLDING CHAIR

Giancarlo Piretti

Giancarlo Piretti

The most difficult aspect to consider when designing folding furniture, especially folding chairs, is the relationship of the folding mechanism, primarily a mechanical function, to the overall design. Designers either try to overcome this mechanism by aesthetic means or settle for a design which is unstable, due to over-simplification. In both cases, the design aberrations have an immediate impact on price. On the one hand, the chair designed for temporary use soars in price because of decorative or structural incongruities; on the other, the chair is so cheaply made that the sitter's use is compromised by poor functional quality. All of these considerations pose a serious challenge to the designer.

Giancarlo Piretti's "Plia" folding chair is different. For the Plia, dating from 1969, is more than a chair that can be folded: it is *the* folding chair *par excellence*. It is inexpensive and space-saving, the folding mechanism is clearly visible, and it can be used both indoors and outdoors. The core element of this chair is a hinge with three metal discs. These are part of two rectangular frames and one U-shaped hoop, which form the backrest and front support, the seat and the rear support. The perfect mechanism makes it possible not only to fold these three components into a single compact unit, whose maximum thickness is a mere 5 centimetres, but also to stack the chair when folded.

Piretti's Plia chair made design history because it was one of the most ingenious folding chairs ever. Many contemporaries, for example the Grand Dame of Italian design—Isa Vercelloni—saw this design as "a product predestined to stand as the image of an era." This does not seem to be an exaggeration. For, thanks to the rounded edges and corners, the round, concave seating hollow and, last but not least, the choice of materials (polished aluminium frame, transparent plastic), the Plia folding chair achieves a Pop Art character of downright pictographic precision. It is notable that the formal insignia do not serve any obvious decorative purpose but are instead functional and structural throughout.   V.A.

Ingenious folding mechanism: the Plia chair collapses to a mere 5-centimetre width.

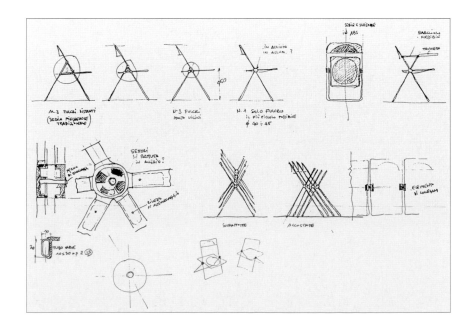

Design sketches by Giancarlo Piretti.

OLIVETTI VALENTINE TYPEWRITER
Ettore Sottsass

Ettore Sottsass

1917   Born on September 14 in Innsbruck, Austria
1935–39 Studies at the Turin Politecnico
1947   Sets up his own studio in Milan; active in the areas of architecture, painting, ceramics, jewellery, furniture and tapestries
1950–55 Architecture projects for the post-war reconstruction of northern Italian cities commissioned by an insurance firm
1956   Works for George Nelson, New York
1958–80 Design consultant for Olivetti
1959   Receives the Compasso d'Oro for the Elea 9003 electronic calculator
1960   Own office in Milan
1970   Honorary doctorate from the Royal College of Art, London
1972   Begins design work for Alessi
1975   Founding member of the Global Tools group
1978–79 Works for Studio Alchimia
1980   Founds the atelier Sottsass Associati together with Aldo Cibic, Matteo Thun and Marco Zanini; interiors for Fiorucci; corporate identity for Esprit and Alessi
1981–85 Founding member of the Memphis group
1986   Founds the Italiana di Communicazione advertising agency

The portable Valentine typewriter is a perfect example of the provocative power of Italian design. The device consists of two parts: the typewriter itself and the hard plastic carrying case into which it can be pushed or lowered for storage or transportation. Machine and box together form a whole: therein lie both the provocation and the innovation. Previously—for example under Marcello Nizzoli, who created lasting design masterpieces for Olivetti—the machine had always been a piece unto itself. In order to make the typewriter portable, a separate case or bag was required. Now the values seemed inverted: when in use, the Valentine is only a part, but in its case it becomes a whole. This was functional design that focused on the perspective of non-use rather than use. The public greeted this subversive gesture with glee.

The rear panel of the typewriter, which doubles as the lid for the box, is equipped with a carrying handle. The shape of the Valentine is defined from the "rear": the rear panel is the "base panel." The front—mocking the unlucky writer struck by writer's block—is relatively insignificant by comparison. Once again, we find an exact reversal of established rules and values. The front of the Valentine is cut off at an angle, leaving the keys to stand freely. The key levers are protected by a bar shaped like the car bumper on a contemporary Volvo safety model. The overall appearance of the machine and the cross-section of the housing announce that this machine is lowered into, or pulled out of a plastic box. Notches on the bottom, designed to catch the guiding mechanism in the box, and two plastic clasps on the lid create a complete fit between machine and box. Photographs of the two elements just before the box is closed are reminiscent of coupling and uncoupling manoeuvres in space. The red colour of the Valentine, another affront to ergonomic and functional design principles (generally pastel colours in the green or grey range were used to prevent eye fatigue), offered an unexpected, welcomed boldness.   C.L.

An amusing advertisement for the Valentine featuring a detail from a painting by Piero di Cosimo.

The bright red, portable typewriter captured the 1960s *zeitgeist*.

The Valentine: a sporty work companion, whether on the beach or in a café.

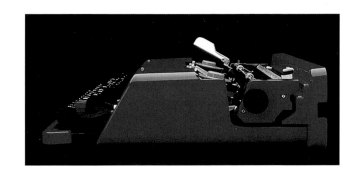

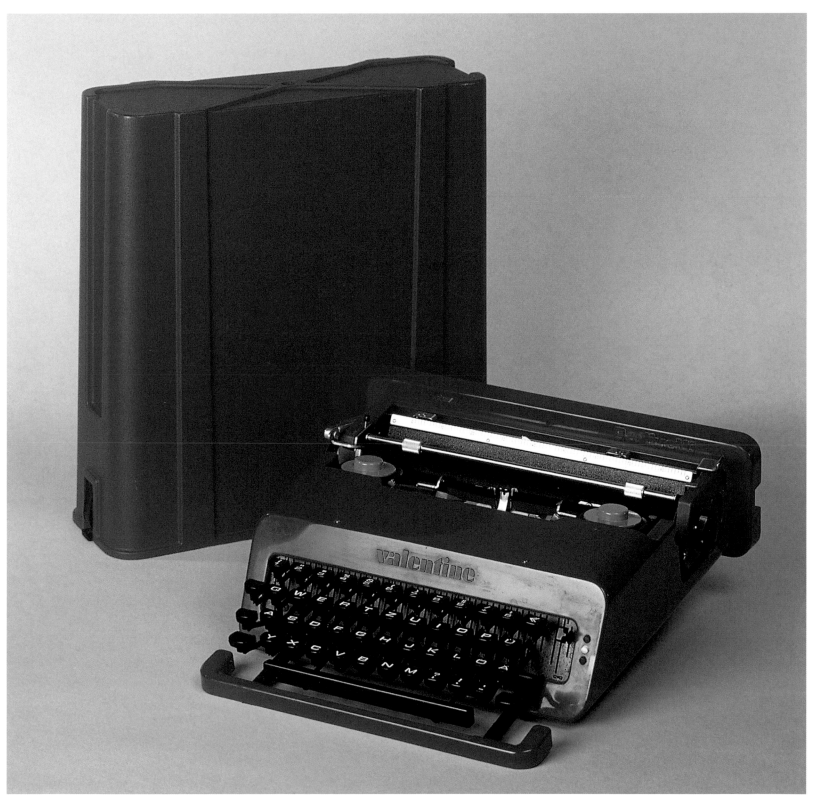

B&O BEOGRAM 4000

Jacob Jensen

Designing a turntable presents two problems. Technically, how can you keep the cartridge tracking reliably in a record's grooves? Aesthetically, if you adhere to the ideals of modernism, how can you reduce the turntable's forms and action to geometric simplicity? The Beogram 4000's designers resolved these difficulties with considerable intelligence and imagination.

Engineer Subir K. Pramanik wanted to create a turntable that was isolated from the vibrations of the world around it. He was intrigued by the possibility of making a tone arm that tracked a record's grooves tangentially, at a constant angle. He also suggested the use of a light and two photocells to control the tone arm. Krebs Soerensen developed the electronics for controlling the tone arm. Later, consultant Gustav Zeuthen built a prototype which solved a number of problems that had arisen during the development of the design, while Jensen suggested a second arm to emphasize tangential tracking. Soerensen mounted a light on that inner arm, which detected the size of the record album and adjusted the turntable's speed accordingly.

Jensen styled a housing for the Beogram 4000 that both continued and advanced Bang & Olufsen's understated, refined approach to hi-fi design. The Beogram 4000's aluminium surface, with its flush-mounted controls, is nicely offset by the wood that frames the bottom section of the turntable. Whether the plastic cover is raised or lowered, the turntable retains an Euclidean purity which is undisturbed when the machine is working. The platter is a circle, its surrounding housing a rectangle. The paired arms—one for detecting the record's size, the other for the needle to play the record—remain parallel to the sides of the turntable as the record plays. Geometric order is maintained at rest and in motion.

When one starts the Beogram, a small light on the inner arm turns on, beaming downwards. The light arm and toner arm move towards the record, and as the beam reaches the first grooves of the album the sequence begins. The toner arm follows the light arm and lightly sets onto the record at precisely the right place.

The Beogram 4000's sturdy case ensures that once the stylus is in contact with the record album only a very significant shock will pop it off. According to Pramanik, you can put the 4000 on a table, start playing a record on it and pound on the table repeatedly without knocking the stylus out of place. In the realm of stereo equipment, manufacturers often create components so as to show off advances (real or imagined), regardless of an integrated design. Bang & Olufsen's team took another route, introducing a significant innovation while continuing the firm's tradition of elegant form.   T.D.S.

Sleek and elegant: hi-fi technology combined with a timeless design in the Beogram.

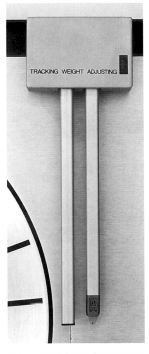

The Beogram's innovative tone arm emphasized its tangential tracking.

TIZIO TABLE LAMP

Richard Sapper

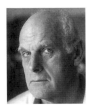

Richard Sapper

1932   Born on May 30 in Munich, Germany
1952–56 Studies philosophy, graphic design and
          mechanical engineering; degree in busi-
          ness administration from the University
          of Munich
1956–58 Works in the design department of
          Daimler-Benz, Stuttgart
1958   Moves to Italy; works in the atelier of
          Gio Ponti, Milan; later works for the
          La Rinascente store chain
1959   Works on the Italian translation of
          Paul Klee's diaries (together with
          Mario Spagnol)
1959–75 Collaboration with Marco Zanuso
1968   Organizes (with Pio Manzù and William
          Lansing Plumb) an exhibition for the four-
          teenth Milan Triennale
1970–76 Consultant for Fiat and Pirelli for test
          cars and car accessories
1972   Founds a studio with Gae Aulenti for new
          forms of local public mass transportation
1978   Begins projects for Alessi
1980   Industrial design consultant to IBM
1985   Teaches summer courses for Yale Univer-
          sity in Brisaggo
1986–98 Professor of industrial design at the
          Academy of Fine Arts, Stuttgart
1988   Honorary member of the Royal Society of
          Arts, London

Sapper's Tizio lamp is among the key cult objects of the 1980s and 1990s. Its skeletal, insect-like, almost predatory form hovers over desks and tables in fashionable, modern interiors worldwide. Born in Germany, but having spent much of his working life in Italy, the product designer Richard Sapper succeeded—in this and other designs—to combine the rational functionality of the modern German design philosophy with the elegance and sculptural integrity of Italy's best-known, post-war designs. This German-Italian link lies at the very heart of the Tizio lamp. Made of ABS plastic and aluminium, and rendered in matte black, it is a highly engineered product. The lamp's subtle workings are concealed but result in a sense of magic as the user finds that it can rest in any position required; the slightest touch will serve to reposition it. It is this tactile likeability, combined with its harmonious, minimal appearance, that explains its widespread appeal. Subtle details—such as the red switch and red highlights at the key joints, together with perforations that allow light and heat to emanate from the casings—are both practical and aesthetic at the same time.

Designed in 1972, the Tizio was created at the peak of Sapper's creative career. Prior to setting up his own studio in Germany in 1970, he had worked closely with the Italian designer Marco Zanuso on a number of stunningly original product designs of the 1960s, among them the little folding radio of 1964 for Brionvega—the TS-502 (see p. 134)—and the all-black, minimal Algol television set for the same company. With Zanuso, he evolved an approach to design which combined the aesthetic with the functional while never letting one dominate the other. His gift lies in concealing the mechanisms of his objects without giving the impression of there being a superficial shell which does not contribute to the function. The Tizio's slim structure with its balances, weighted base and minimal hood, that conceals its low voltage halogen bulb, all work together in a visually integrated manner, seeming to illuminate without the necessary electrical wiring and connections. It has the integrity of a single, organic whole. The user engages only with the upper arm and the switch, the rest of the elements just being there, necessary parts of the whole.

Sapper's work reached wide audiences in the 1980s. It was appreciated by a large number of design-conscious consumers who sought stylish objects that functioned well. Among his greatest successes was his Bollitore kettle for Alessi, which quickly became a cult object *par excellence*. More often on display than in actual use, its rounded metal form and coxcomb detail brought a touch of humour into an otherwise highly serious oeuvre. The Tizio lamp remains as popular as ever and shows no signs of being superseded.   P.S.

The precursor to the Tizio
helped determine the
necessary counterweights.

The Tizio has outgrown its desk life:
it is not only quality lighting but a
symbol of modern lifestyle.

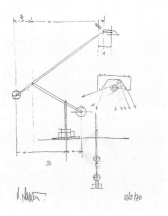

Richard Sapper's design
sketch for the Tizio.

SONY WALKMAN
Sony Design Centre

The introduction of the cassette tape in 1965 was a milestone in user-friendly recording and listening devices. Instead of awkwardly spooling in large tapes, all one needed to do was pop in a cassette, where the beginning and end of the tape no longer mattered in terms of handling. The magnetic tape became mobile: within a few years, listening to music from a cassette tape, for example in the car, became a standard practice.

But this was simply a portable cassette recorder and still a far cry from the groundbreaking "Walkman." Its development and release onto the market is said to have sprung from a family scene in the home of Sony president Akio Morita (1921–1999). He was so annoyed by the constant music played by his teenage children that he devised the idea of outfitting a listening device with headphones only. Since the 1970s, Sony has produced very lightweight headphones with excellent sound qualities used, among other things, for dictation machines.

The Sony Walkman was developed from the "Pressman" dictation machine. In total, the housing for the stereo section and batteries measured a mere 14 by 9 by 2.8 centimetres. Lightweight and small enough to be worn or carried, it could be slipped into a pocket or attached to a belt. It was also shock-proof, thus ideal for jogging.

The housing consisted of blue anodized aluminium, a colour reminiscent of blue jeans, leisure and fun, as was the name Walkman. The sophisticated design, typical of Sony at the time, communicated professional quality. The Walkman delivered music within a protective sphere, accompanying the wearer wherever he or she travelled. In its way, the Walkman changed the relationship between individual and society; it undermined the established order of rules and obedience, prohibition or overstepping of boundaries. Its users sidestepped rules—such as not being allowed to listen to music in public parks because this might disturb others. Instead of music, all that could be heard when standing next to someone with a Walkman was the pounding of the bass.　　　　　　　　　　　　　　　　　　　　　C.L.

Clean design in metallic pastel colours: Sony combined state-of-the-art technology with the fashion sensibilities of the 1980s.

Advertising campaigns for the Sony Walkman promised carefree leisure time, whether on the ski slopes or the beach.

PHILIPS COMPACT DISC

Maestro Herbert von Karajan with one of the first mass-produced compact discs.

At the beginning of the 1970s, it seemed hardly possible to stem the advance of Japanese consumer electronics. American industry seemed to have given up, and even the Dutch firm, Philips, was having problems. This development was reinforced by the economic downturn and the influence of the oil crisis. Moreover, unbridled mass consumption was coming under criticism in reports by the Club of Rome. Just as in the 1930s, when the newly arrived radio played a major part in the recovery from the Great Depression, a search was begun for new products to interest consumers. Philips, which had always had a strong position in the development of professional products, applied its strengths to the invention of new consumer electronics.

In the 1960s, Philips was busy developing instructional equipment for use in education. One of its developments was a programmable audio-visual system combining a cine-projector with a compact cassette recorder. The physics laboratory at Philips was asked whether it could develop a faster, better system. Early experiments used microscopically small film images, recorded with their associated sounds and control signals in a spiral track on a disc. In 1972, Philips came up with a video disc in which laser light was beamed at a spiral track of microscopically small pits impressed on a disc. The pattern of pits contained all the information necessary to allow sound and pictures to be recorded and played back. The first discs were capable of containing around 45,000 images, each of which could be accessed extremely rapidly by means of an index number. By displaying these images at a rate of 25 a second, it was possible to record a half-hour film, and, later, this increased to a full hour.

However, the introduction of the system onto the consumer market in 1978 was too slow. Not enough video discs were available, and the video cassette had already established a strong market position. But the superior quality of the video disc system revealed its potential for educational applications and for creating records of museum collections. In recent years, the video disc has experienced a revival as a recording medium for computer games.

During the development of the video disc, it was discovered that the same technique also made it possible to achieve outstanding sound reproduction. Experiments in 1974 already indicated that there was the potential to eliminate the gramophone record, which itself dated back to the beginning of the century. In 1978, Philips introduced the revolutionary compact disc (CD) to an amazed world that had become accustomed to the limitations of the gramophone record, such as its susceptibility to scratching and fingerprints and its short playing time of half an hour at most.

After its costly experiences in establishing a world standard for the music cassette and a video system, Philips sought the cooperation of the Japanese firm, Sony. In 1980, the Philips CD, a plastic disc measuring 12 centimetres in diameter, became the world standard, initially containing 60—and later 75—minutes' of music. Since then, many versions have appeared, each with its own application; for example, a CD can now be erased and re-recorded. The CD is not a product in the traditional sense of the word. It has opened the way to a whole range of new electronic products in which dematerialization and digital data processing play major roles.   R. K.

The first CD player was introduced onto the market in Japan in 1982 and, a year later, Europe.

IN-LINE SKATES

In-line skates: the American term has become ubiquitous, although some amusing expressions have sprung up in other languages, such as the German *Rollkufen* (rolling blades). In the 1990s, in-line skates were the financial success of the sporting goods industry around the world, with annual growth rates of close to 50 per cent. And the background story of in-line skates reads just like a fairytale. Once upon a time, circa 1980, there were two brothers in Minnesota—Scott and Brennan Olson—who were passionate hockey players. They longed to glide on skates not only in winter, and roller skates in the summertime were not as satisfying as the control and speed achieved on ice. So, the brothers constructed skates that were similar to those designed by a Belgian named Merlin, one hundred years earlier: they arranged several wheels in one line, like a skate, and attached them to shoesoles. While the idea was not new, it was the right idea at the right time! The skateboard, a board on wheels on which young people surf through urban landscapes, showing off their acrobatics, had prepared the ground, so to speak. In-line skaters, too, need the smooth surfaces that are primarily found in cities. But more than anything else, the Olsons enjoyed the benefit of more sophisticated technology. There were now hard-wearing bearings for the wheels, which in turn were both nonabrasive and shock-absorbing; the frame no longer needed to be constructed from metal because lightweight plastics had become available. And to top it all off, the "skate" could be designed in a shape that was reminiscent of both a downhill ski boot and the carapace of an alien.

The Olson brothers called their invention "Rollerblades," now a label used by Benetton. Today, there are many manufacturers. You can buy skates for a few hundred dollars or a cheap model for less than fifty; there are fitness skates, leisure skates, speed skates, all-terrain skates, hockey skates, stunt skates and skates that snap off a running shoe with a simple click. There are associated helmets, knee-, elbow- and wristguards, backpacks, fashion, music, specialist and technical literature, maps and city maps specially produced for in-line skaters. City streets are cordoned off for huge crowds of recreational skaters and competitions abound: marathon races, stunt shows and gladiator fights with blonde beauties pushing each other off the track—all on in-line skates. The real attraction of in-line skates lies less in the shoes or skates themselves or in their technical details. In-line skates increase mobility, but, above all, they promote a contemporary body language: a light and casual style that expresses life in the fast lane, somewhat sexy but also prone to brutality at any moment— namely when the in-line skater hits an obstacle. H.-H.P.

On the move—in-line skates became a popular, new mode of transportation in the mid-1990s.

(below, left to right)

The first in-line skates had a stopper reminiscent of the earlier roller skates.

This model features the new rear brakes.

The "Nature" model has detachable wheels.

This model features a fifth wheel for more speed.

The "Persus alpha" model sports a futuristic design.

CARLTON SIDEBOARD
Ettore Sottsass

Perhaps no other work by Ettore Sottsass reveals this designer's approach more clearly than his 1981 *Mobile divisorio*, known as the Carlton sideboard or bookshelf. Already in 1976, at an exhibition in Berlin, Sottsass postulated "that there is no design solution that could not rightfully be 'another' solution, and should this be more or less true, what mattered was to initiate a method of designing with the focus less on 'perfect' form, the ideal form or the idea of form, than on the 'method of searching for form.'"

Indeed, none of the characteristics normally associated with such a functional piece of furniture, often referred to as a bookshelf, are present. The Carlton is heavy and almost obtrusively dominant. The tiers, to be utilized as shelves, are loud and colourful. Some are U-shaped or trapezoidal, others triangular; some are set at an angle, and others are open towards the sides. There is not a hint of distilled functionality, of exclusively "practical" usability! But those were not Sottsass's concerns. His Carlton, a design for the first collection of the Memphis Group, which he co-founded in 1980, had one primary goal: to point to a new direction away from utilitarian functionalism, which at that time had become frozen self-reference. "Memphis's function is to exist," he once replied when asked about the function of the group. Consequently, this bookshelf did not embody anything completely new, nor did any of the other works by this group. Rather, it was a model, suggesting the multiplicity of stylistic possibilities in the design of such a piece of furniture.

The deep-rooted scepticism towards the formula "form follows function" expressed here was not entirely new, having emerged already in the late 1950s and early 1960s. While kidney shapes or adherence to the infallibility of the grid prevailed elsewhere, Sottsass had long since formulated a different point of departure for his reasoning: the interrelationship between human beings and their environment determined by intuition, ritual and emotion. Hence, for Sottsass, furniture, objects, houses or mere details featured in large or small architecture were, and are, not simply accessories for show, but are functional aspects that can surprise the world. They are clues and reference points, expressions of an individually developed personality that has taken on form.   V.A.

With its colourful patchwork of laminate surfaces and expansive shapes, the Carlton should be seen as a rebellion against functionalism.

Ettore Sottsass
Biography see p. 140

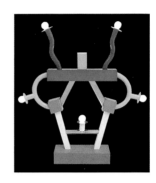

THE FACE

Neville Brody

Neville Brody

1957   Born in London
1975   Studies painting at Hornsey College,
           London
1976   Studies at the London College of
           Printing; designs record sleeves
1981–86 Graphic designer for *The Face*

The London-based, monthly style journal *The Face* was launched in May 1980 by music journalist Nick Logan. As the most widely known of several independent publications (including *Blitz* and *ID*) produced to reflect and influence the energy of those young urban style movements which fed innovation into the fields of British music, design and fashion post-punk, *The Face* came to represent the cultural tenor of that decade.

Neville Brody, a graphic designer trained at the London College of Printing was employed to lend the magazine its distinctive visual identity between 1981 and 1986. Brody's interest in the history of his medium resulted in layouts that drew directly from the aesthetic concerns of Russian Constructivists such as El Lissitzky (1890–1941) and Alexander Rodchenko (1891–1956), whilst subverting their political messages. He deliberately deconstructed the rigid grids used by more traditional, glossy fashion magazines, such as *Vogue*, against which *The Face* based its feel and approach. Asymmetrical typography and arcane symbols in bold primary colours, set in competing self-invented fonts and mixed point sizes, were used to frame equally challenging fashion images in grainy monochrome. Homoerotic and sadomasochistic signifiers by avant-garde photographers and stylists such as Nick Knight and Ray Petri, or polemical articles on subjects as diverse as subcultural dressing, inner-city poverty, club music and new technologies, were regular features. A certain fluidity between the look of the magazine, its editorial direction, its advertising and its visual language allowed the reader to "surf" its content in a new way, reconstructing both the idea of a fashion magazine and its relationship with its audience. The readers' letters page suggested a vibrant dialogue between staff writers and designers and the magazine's audience, setting the question of authorship into some dispute. This has given rise to several claims that *The Face* was a truly postmodern medium, impossible to categorize and infuriatingly evasive in terms of its relationship to the social inequalities associated with the rise of consumerism in the 1980s, but unavoidably authoritative in its self-consciously "cool" assessment of the popular culture of the period.

From the mid-1980s onwards, and following Brody's departure from its staff, *The Face* lost its eclectic and rather dangerous edge. It opened itself up to advertising from elite and global fashion brands and became more closely associated with the lifestyle choices of affluent young metropolitan professionals. By the end of the decade, its strong individualist voice had become the possession of Condé Nast publishers. Similarly, the graphic language which Brody pioneered had by now gone on to influence a range of competitors and found its distinctive forms appropriated in the commercial field, used as packaging for everything from shampoo to compact discs. The championing of Brody by the mainstream was marked by a major exhibition devoted to his work, held at the Victoria and Albert Museum in 1988, whilst the look of the magazine became more reticent and classical in its references. Nevertheless, *The Face* has survived for 20 years as a leader in the field and has marked out a territory in which countless younger style journals have been able to thrive.   C.B.

Risqué topics and an avant-garde layout make *The Face* into a trend-setter in every respect.

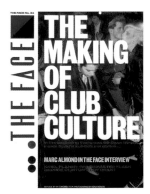

A retrospective at the Victoria and Albert Museum was organized on the occasion of the fiftieth issue of *The Face*.

Neville Brody's ingenious treatment of typography and provocative photography gave *The Face* its edge.

COSTES CHAIR
Philippe Starck

If plagiarism, number of copies or paraphrases were unmistakable indicators of quality in design, then Philippe Starck's Costes chair would undoubtedly be one of the greatest of its kind. Designers of every persuasion, from home-decorating chains and proponents of post-modernism to successful mainstream designers, have used the important model invented by Starck in 1982. In that same year, the owner of the Café Costes saw this chair exhibited at the VIA Gallery in Paris. Two years later, in 1984, Starck was commissioned to design the interior of this Paris café, which featured the chair, now known as the Costes chair.

Such repeated borrowing of an original idea is not unusual, but it seems amusing in this instance because Starck's design, too, must be understood as a quotation, a reference to an established predecessor. But Starck's true mastery reveals itself in his creative treatment of such a model, setting him apart from mainstream imitators. While the designs of the latter strive as far as possible to maintain the hip aura of the original—through minute changes to the construction, overall shape or surface, for obvious, primarily financial reasons—Starck's chair can be described confidently as a complex reinterpretation of an ancient form known even in antiquity. This new interpretation does not have just a formal basis, that is, the comprehensive trimming down of every component; it is also rooted in the rigorous treatment of composition and construction with a view to mass production.

Despite all its historical allusions to the classic armchair, Starck's Costes chair is extremely simple. And if its tubular frame and slightly oval shell were not discreetly varnished or lacquered in black, the obvious materiality would compel one to speak of a brutalistic concept. However, the Olympian rise to prominence of the Costes chair is a direct result of the graphic translatability of its image. There is perhaps no other chair that so readily communicates the manufacturer's name, Driade, the author's name and the advantages of comfortable, drawing room-style sitting. The chair embodies the myth of Paris, the quintessential metropolis.   V.A.

Philippe Starck

1949	Born on January 18 in Paris
1965–67	Studies at the Nissim de Camondo School
1969	Founds a firm for inflatable houses; "Spanish" chair
1971–72	Art décorateur for Pierre Cardin
1973	Begins work as interior designer
1976	Interior design for the La main bleue nightclub, Paris
1979	Founds Starck Products company
1983–84	Furnishes the Elysée Palace, Paris
1984	Interior design for the Café Costes, Paris; begins a furniture collection for the French mail-order company, Les 3 Suisses
1985	Expands his company to include architecture and industrial design; teaches at the Domus Academy, Milan
1985–87	La Moult House, Paris
1987	Teaches at the Ecole des Arts Décoratifs, Paris
1988	Begins collaboration with Alberto Alessi
1989	Nani Nani biomorphic building with restaurant, exhibition space and offices for the Rikugo Company, Tokyo
1989–90	Administration building for the Asahi Brewery, Tokyo
1993	Groningen Museum (together with Alessandro Mendini, Coop Himmelblau and Michele de Lucchi)
1994	Starck House, also as instruction kit for the construction of a wooden house, for Les 3 Suisses

In the 1980s, Café Costes was the place to be seen.

SWATCH WATCH

By the beginning of the 1980s, the Japanese watch industry's reputation as a plagiarist and producer of poor-quality watches was disappearing. Its inexpensive, mass-produced, electronic digital watches kept good time and could be bought almost anywhere—so that they were even threatening the Swiss watch industry. Nicolas Hayek, Czech by origin, took on the Japanese challenge by bringing out the Delirium, the world's thinnest electronic watch. He collected around him a group of specialists from various disciplines. The resulting "Swatch" concept (the name was formed by joining the words Swiss and Watch) meant a complete break with the obsolete, moribund Swiss watch industry. His approach necessitated radical reorganization and the integration of a number of different companies, but it seemed to offer the only hope of rescuing the Swiss watch industry.

His aim was to develop a completely new watch with an entirely new marketing concept, and one that ensured capable mass production. The watch was to be a robust, watertight, electronic wristwatch, which would keep good time and be affordable. As a symbolic gesture to traditional Swiss precision and reliability, the watch would not be digital but analogue, with hands. It all sounded very logical, but it meant finding an enormous number of new technical solutions. The movement was regulated by the regular, electronically stimulated oscillation of a quartz crystal. The usual number of components was reduced from well over 100 to no more than 54. The case was a miracle of precision engineering and moulding technology. The assembly was completely automated and took place in a factory hermetically sealed against prying eyes and employing only a very few people. The components and even the glass were no longer attached by small screws but fixed together using ultrasonics. One result was that a Swatch would be impossible to repair; it would always be cheaper to buy a new one.

Every Swatch is exactly the same: only the face and the strap offer any opportunity for design. Every year since the Swatch was introduced, the Swatch Design Lab in Milan has designed around 70 new versions, using such designers as Franco Bosisio, Alessandro Mendini and Matteo Thun. The Swatch has completely changed the image of the traditional watch. From being a timepiece, it has become a fashion accessory for all, regardless of social status. It closely follows fashion and the changing interests of the consumer, but its high quality and reliability mean that it has never become a disposable item like so many other mass-produced products. Indeed, there are collectors, auctions and a whole range of publications keenly following developments in the Swatch. Since the 1990s, there have been a series of extensions to the original Swatch range, including an automatic version with no battery, the Chrono-Swatch, the Diver's Swatch, the Pop Swatch and a number of more expensive versions with additional features.

R.K.

Special artist editions have enriched the Swatch line, such as the collection designed by American artist Keith Haring.

The colourful, large, round Pop Swatch has an elastic fabric wristband.

Swiss technology, clever design and
low price: the classic models of the first
Swatch collection from 1983.

APPLE MACINTOSH
Hartmut Esslinger and Frogdesign

Hartmut Esslinger

1944	Born on June 5 in Beuren, Germany
1966–67	Studies electrical engineering at the Technical University, Stuttgart
1968–70	Studies industrial design at the College for Design in Schwäbisch Gmünd
1969	Opens his first design office in Altensteig together with two partners
1970	Color 3020 television set for Wega-Radio, Fellbach
1973	"Tribel" adjustable shower head for Hansgrohe, Schiltach
1975–76	Concept 51 K audio system for Wega
1979	"Froller" roller skate for Indusco, Auburn Heights, Michigan; Trinitron television set for Sony, Tokyo
1981	"Allegroh" faucet for Hansgrohe
1982	Opens a design office in Campbell, California
1982–85	Works exclusively for Apple Computers, Cupertino, California; designs products including the Macintosh computer (1984)
1986	Opens an office in Tokyo (in 1991 this office moves to Singapore)
1986–93	Sanitary ware for Villeroy & Boch
1987	II GS computer for Apple Computers
1988	Computer system for NeXT, United States
1989	Liom camera for Olympus, Japan; Magic line pans for Fissler, Germany; starts working for Logitech, Fremont, California, designing such items as the logo (1989) and the "Mouse Man" computer mouse (1990)
1989–91	Office furniture for COR, Rheda-Wiedenbrück
1990	Opens an office in Taipei, Taiwan; answering machine for AT&T
1995	"Scenic" computer system for Siemens, Germany
1996	Redesigns Lufthansa terminals, Frankfurt
1997	Cruise ship for the Walt Disney Company, Burbank, California
1999	Redesigns R/3 software for SAP, Germany/United States; "Clio" mini-notebook for Vadem, United States

Products in the communications technology sector seldom become classics. Often, processor speed—a characteristic of short-lived products—prevents the breadth of experience and range of interpretation necessary over the course of decades as prerequisites for this status. This is different with the Apple Macintosh, since innovation here in user logistics made room for an equally important innovation in design. The prerequisite for the machine called a "personal computer" (PC) was the development, in the late 1970s and early 1980s, of chip capacities that could execute several million mathematical operations. In 1976, Steven Paul Jobs and Stephen G. Wozniak founded the Apple Computer Company. Their first product still resembled a travelling typewriter, but, by 1977, their first computer, the Apple II, entered the market with a colour monitor and a separate keyboard. In 1981, the Apple III followed with an integrated floppy disk drive. That same year, the one-millionth Apple II was produced. Then, in 1984, the Apple Macintosh was introduced. This PC, Mac for short, quickly became the standard of the entire computer family. Repeatedly reworked, while remaining principally true to its original form for nearly ten years until the end of 1993, the computer became a symbol of a hitherto unknown user-oriented symbiosis between hardware and software. This paradigm shift lay in the fact that the user became of equal rank with the then-dominating computer specialists. At the beginning of the 1980s, Steven Jobs launched a design competition among eight, primarily European, design offices, with Hartmut Esslinger clearly winning the competition. For the first time, Frogdesign created a snow-white computer that clearly stood out from the dreary brown-beige boxes *à la* IBM. Therefore, not only could the dynamic nature and corporate identity of the company be successfully visualized, but the ensemble of monitor, keyboard and mouse became the creative ideal, above all for the culturally sensitized working processes of architects, graphic designers, product designers and advertising agencies. The graphic resolution and software performance, too, possessed a quality hard to match by competitors. The user desktop represented the office environment. With the introduction of the PageMaker program in 1985, professional layout design with text, graphics and images became a reality for the layperson. Although the incompatible Microsoft Windows world has grown dominant in the meantime, the Mac remains attractive in Europe, primarily for graphically oriented professions, while being promoted in the United States as the "computer for everyone."

With its colourful casings in translucent plastic, the iMac is a perfect expression of design trends of the 1990s.

Recently, with its translucent, candy-coloured iMacs and eMates, Apple has once again set the standard for design. The two main operating systems—Macintosh from Apple on the one hand and MS-DOS, or Windows, from Microsoft on the other—still split users into two groups competing with near-religious conviction and fervour. Hence, the step to full compatibility between the two software systems seems long overdue. Yet, the creative power, indeed Esslinger's ingenious invention of snow-white boxes, is in no way injurious. Apple, the Mac and Frog are a dialectical success story with the whole representing far more than the sum of its component parts. V.F.

The Apple Macintosh:
one of the most popular
of the early models.

MOTOROLA MICROTAC

Rudy Krolopp, Al Nagele and Leon Soren

On April 3, 1973, Motorola engineer Martin Cooper pressed a red button on a DynaTAC telephone and began the first cellular phone call. Cooper later told *The New York Times* that he placed his first cellular call to the then-head of research at Bell Labs, part of AT&T and Motorola's competitor for the nascent wireless market. The Bell Labs chief informed *The Times* that he does not remember the call. The 38.4-ounce prototype DynaTAC, nicknamed "the brick," seems halfway between a Second World War walkie-talkie and a cordless phone of circa 1990. But as the first portable cellular phone, it was a great step forward, and the first installment of significant Motorola innovations.

Motorola slowly reduced the size and weight of its phones, until it achieved a drastic weight reduction with its 1989 MicroTAC cellular telephone, the first "flip phone." At the urging of cellular design chief Rudy Krolopp, Motorola designers Al Nagele and Leon Soren had come up with a groundbreaking innovation: a space-saving flip form that became a visual paradigm. Users flipped the MicroTAC's mouthpiece open to begin and answer calls and flipped it closed to end their conversations. The compact design and light weight (10.7 ounces) of the MicroTAC made it possible to keep close at hand at almost all times. The flip-down mouthpiece provided a measure of privacy for those holding phone conversations in public places. (Whether some cellular users really want to keep their telephone discussions private is another matter.)

Dan Williams, Krolopp's successor, together with Nagele and Soren set out to make Motorola's next major cellular phone "wearable." Further advances in the miniaturization of batteries and electric circuitry—and in Motorola's divisions that produce those components—aided the designers in their goal. In creating the new phone, the Motorola team wanted to keep the popular flip feature but struggled to find a way to make a balanced design. One proposed prototype divided the phone into two segments that would fold into one, like a clam. Nagele suggested placing the battery and earpiece together on one side of a "clam" design, opposite the keypad and mouthpiece. This was a radical step; some at the firm doubted that power could be reliably transmitted across the phone's hinge. Motorola senior managers were so deeply impressed by the superiority of the design, they persuaded their engineers to execute it.

In 1996, Motorola introduced their new phone—the StarTAC. Its elegant design springs from the desire to be functional, beautiful and memorable, and it achieves all three of these aims. While the phone is not the product of a rigorous aesthetic, it reveals what can be achieved when designers (and their managers) remain open to possibilities. Motorola gained a great deal by assiduously trying to make less of its cellular phones. In the StarTAC, less is much more.   T.D.S

A 1997 model with an elegant shell design.

(right)
The folding mechanism of the MicroTAC revolutionized the shape of cell phones.

Smaller, lighter and more portable: the rapid development of the cellular phone.

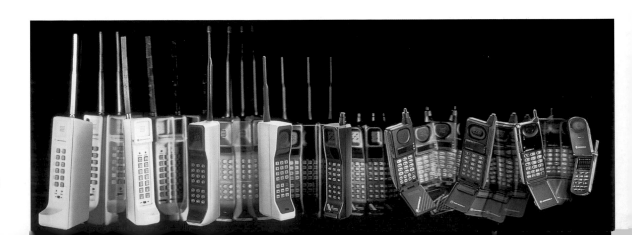

JUICY SALIF

Philippe Starck

Philippe Starck
Biography see p. 157

Design sketch by Philippe Starck.

which is like, that

Philippe Starck's lemon squeezer polarizes opinions. For those who tend to look at design from primarily aesthetic viewpoints, the citrus press is a passionate reference point amid the *tristesse* of monotonous kitchen utensils, a precious jewel in the practical humdrum. Or, conversely, the final proof of consumer behaviour solely dedicated to show, an ultimate symbol of extravagant, jet-setter hedonism.

Opinions are just as divided in the camp of those who evaluate design according to practical, functional criteria. For some, the squeezer is yet another stroke of genius by the French design star, who continuously manages to evade popular expectations. And who, as this model demonstrates, is able not only to create a new interpretation of something as commonplace as the lemon squeezer but achieves this with such convincing simplicity—by isolating the cone and placing it on three legs, perfectly perched above a matching glass. The juice, following the laws of physics, no longer flows through a sieve into a holding dish but straight into the glass. It is that simple—that logical.

Starck was the first to discover this ingenious solution to this everyday kitchen task. No previous designer was able to transcend the traditional approach, the familiar configuration repeated in countless variations on the lemon squeezer: container plus sieve plus squeezer. *Making it unique* Starck's critics, however, attack his creation precisely because it lacks these fundamental parts and grumble about how it processes the fruit. The sieve, they argue, catches the pulp and pits; the container has a shaped spout; the utensil is handier, no pointed legs digging into the work surface, and so on.

One thing is clear: it would be impossible to gather more objectively based arguments either for, or against, this unit. Regardless of which side one favours, whether one pays homage to this design or believes it is rubbish, Starck has clearly succeeded in one regard: manifesting a fundamental paradigm shift in design. The Juicy Salif lemon squeezer, more than any other popular design at the close of the century, has altered the way in which we pose a basic question. Today, the question no longer is "What do we need?" It has become the simple question "What else might we still want?" The Juicy Salif provides one answer. V.A.

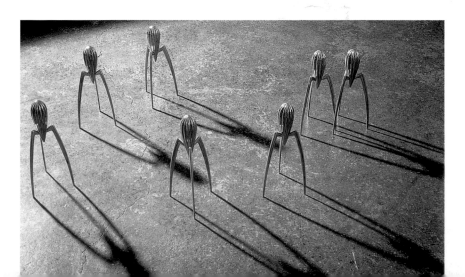

Innovation or nonsense? Opinions are divided when it comes to Philippe Starck's lemon squeezer.

In the 1960s, computer systems of large corporations were linked in the United States to exchange research information. The military, too, made use of such internal networks of large-scale computers, so-called intranets. After the collapse of Communism and the end of the Cold War, the U.S. Defense Department released this technology for general use: within a decade the Internet emerged as the largest computer intranet in the world. In the meantime, more than 80 million people communicate via the worldwide network. The volume of data transmitted on a daily basis currently corresponds to one million books at 200 pages each. Governments, corporations, parties, associations, interest groups and private individuals publish their issues. On-line computers are made internet-capable by means of a modem. They should be equipped with multimedia interfaces in order to fully utilize the capacities of the Net, which increasingly replaces television and telephone, radio and CD-player, computer-game console and CD-Rom.

But more than information and data are exchanged on and through the World Wide Web (WWW). It also provides an environment for business and consumption, entertainment and social life: buying and selling through "e-commerce," conversing and flirting in "chatrooms," handling transactions with "e-banking," making a telephone call with "NetMeeting," sending and receiving letters via "e-mail"; but also watching films, playing computer games, listening to and storing music. Additional peripherals are often required for all this. The Net offers almost any kind of service. The millions of newsgroups on any imaginable topic function like blackboards with posted news. Since anyone can participate in the Internet via a personal computer (PC), it is decentralized, anti-hierarchical, belongs to no one and is thus, by definition, grass roots democracy: no government, no regime, no enterprise can deny or even control access. But if more and more people communicate and work in data nets, if economic and social organizational structures are largely determined by the WWW and cyberspace, then access must be regulated and the rights of the individual defined. Moral standards and controls against criminal misuse are still handled individually by each country.

However, since information—be it commercial or private—can not only be accessed on the Net but also input, websites and homepages each require a name and address, so-called domains, assigned for a fee. Web information can be read not only discursively like a book, but so-called links enable the reader to jump between pages and objects with a click of the mouse, thus travelling through, or "surfing," the Net. For a fee, search engines and on-line services offer access and orientation assistance in the Net, whose huge databanks otherwise would be the equivalent of a mega-library without catalogue. Insofar as design means service, aside from optimizing the utility and significance of objects, and since hardware and software, whose components must be designed, are increasingly a dialectic unit since the digitalization of all areas of life, each individual computer and every computer conglomerate, and thus also the WWW, have become a context that is relevant to design. For millions of websites, their visual quality and professional treatment guarantee that they will be noticed, above all for commercial Internet users. And thus, new professions have sprung up in and around the Net, not only info-scouts, net-trainers or hardware and software net-technicians but also website designers. V.F.

The Internet has no limits: whether it be books, cars, CDs, furniture or watches, almost anything can be accessed and purchased through the World Wide Web.

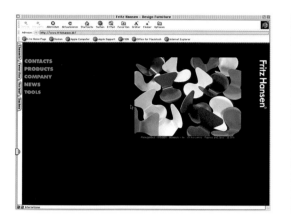

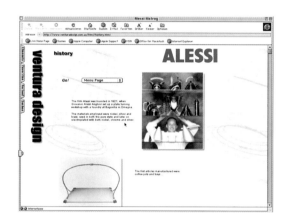

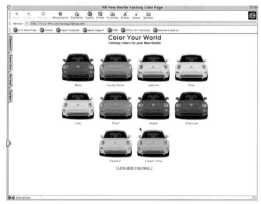

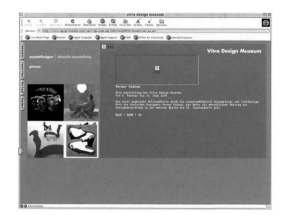

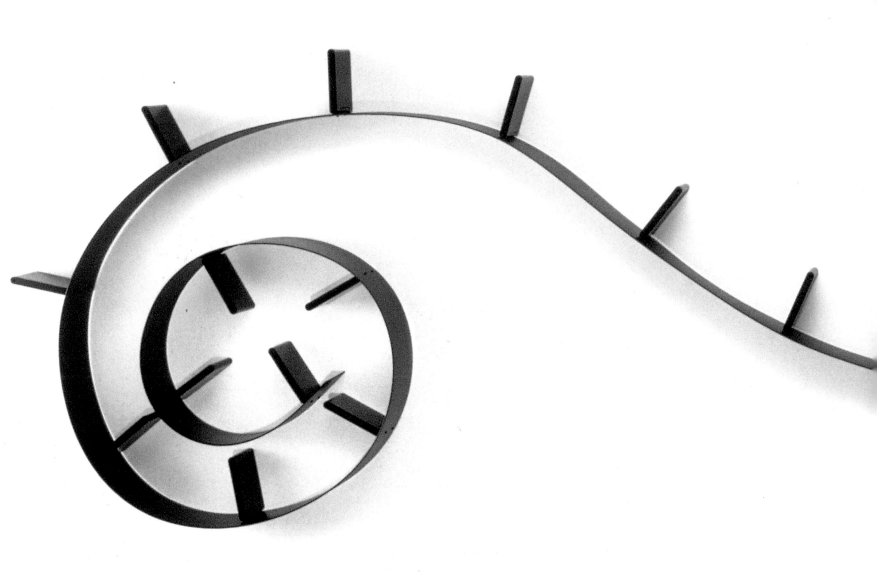

Shelving by the yard: Ron Arad presented the Bookworm in a variety of metal models which proved to be too expensive. The shelving system became a sales hit once the coloured plastic model was introduced in 1994.

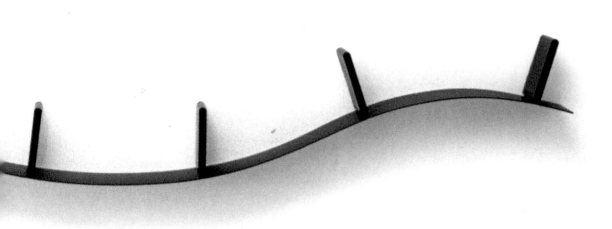

Ron Arad

With the Bookworm shelf, designer Ron Arad reached a level of achievement denied most designers. He successfully introduced a radically new and different formal canon in an area that is defined, more than most, by specific fundamental tenets of form.

At issue is the bookshelf. The very mention of the word evokes an image that is more or less constant: a frame divided into horizontal and vertical planes with the primary function of book storage. There are many variations on the theme. They include diagonal or moveable intermediary supports, attached or loose individual shelves, economy or deluxe versions. All of these variations, however, are characterized by right angles and by the interplay between components arranged within a rectangle. The basic typology of the shelving unit has become at least as conventional as that of the table or chair.

Arad's Bookworm strays from this convention. In fact, it is the antithesis. The Bookworm is not characterized by individual shelves staggered one on top of the other, or by any kind of side attachments. There is a complete absence of definition; all is left to the individual imagination.

The most frequent form of assembly—a sort of stylized S-shape—reflects a kinship with the familiar constructions made from wooden boards or steel sheets. Nevertheless, this particular form of assembly demonstrates the fundamental flexibility of the plastic band which can be supplied in three lengths, instead of one. Hence the S represents just one option of many—it merely demonstrates the intended purpose of this Bookworm and the use of this simple band with upright loops, shaped like books and attached at regular intervals.

It primarily differs from other shelving systems in that it permits the owner to create individually styled versions of the shelving "unit." While the system permits only a specific number of planned constellations, thus laying claim to a certain order, the Bookworm gives the user free rein in how to set it up. The shape of the Bookworm and, with it, the many variations in how books or similar objects are displayed, is dictated only by each individual's personal taste.   V.A.

The Bookworm variations seem endless: the individual elements can be combined into almost any kind of form.

TAMAGOTCHI
Aki Maita

The Tamagotchi, freely translated as "little egg to hold and love," was developed in 1996 by Aki Maita, an employee in the research department of Japanese toy manufacturer, Bandai. The miniaturized, interactive computer toy simulates the care and raising of a pet. A flattened, plastic egg (4 by 5 centimetres) contains a square, liquid-crystal screen no larger than 2 by 2 centimetres, with a pixel capacity of just 16 to 32 dots. A zigzag line surrounds the miniature screen in the guise of a cracked eggshell, beneath which three buttons are arranged in a row. These are used to feed the cyber chick, to play with it, to switch on the light in the "cage" or to clean it out. The top and bottom sections of the screen are reserved for eight symbols which represent different functions of the Tamagotchi, while the centre section forms the virtual pet's cage. Depending on the frequency of the owner's play actions, the "pet" changes during its "lifetime" into twelve different "characters," which are visually differentiated and display positive and negative, "healthy" or "unhealthy," characteristics. Bad behaviour, neglect, decrepitude, fleeing the nest, nest warmth, discipline: the whole arsenal of bringing up—based on choice, law and order or laissez-faire—is simulated, and its result affects the often still infantile "educators," "parents" and "teachers." Tamagotchi's development can be observed from hatching, that is, from birth, to death if the necessary input has been neglected over a longer period of time—the little chick must be constantly cared for, fed and groomed. It can be disciplined, instructed in good behaviour, played with and taught. It "matures," with one Tamagotchi year corresponding to approximately three days. Its maximum age is 99 years or, roughly, 300 days. It is "aware" of day and night and requires sleep. While the Japanese version of the toy "dies" with poor handling, the European and American versions indicate that it has simply returned to its "home planet." The screen then displays a tiny angel with wings. Another chirping creature can be programmed anew.

Within a short time, these virtual, electronic companions gained in popularity, not only with children but also with adults, in Japan and elsewhere. Upon release, 80,000 models of the toy (priced around £10, or $15) were sold in Japan within 3 days. When export sales began after 8 months, 700,000 Tamagotchi had been sold; while supplies lasted, figures rose to 10 million in Germany by mid-1997 and 40 million worldwide by mid-1998. Success is based, on the one hand, on the simulation of natural life processes and, on the other, on the fascination with electronic gadgets. The toy's mobility, low volume, simple design and operation, moderate price, trendiness and fun secured its popularity.

In the wake of Walkmans, Discmans, Gameboys, beepers and pagers, this interactive toy marks the final transition towards investing digital products with emotional values. From the start, the Tamagotchi has represented a completely new product category, the Cyberpet, and has been joined by artificial parrots and dolphins, dogs and cats, owls and dinosaurs. The sensory socialization, in which responsibility is only enacted in a game but can nevertheless trigger real feelings of grief and frustration in case of malfunction, has found as many passionate proponents as opponents. Sociologists, psychologists and teachers estimate that there are now more than 2,000 Tamagotchi Internet sites, including a "cemetery" as well as websites created by militant chick-haters clamouring for the toy's destruction. Although an entire product line has risen around the Tamagotchi, with more than 70 plagiarized models worldwide and merchandizing specialists vying for licences with T-shirt, bag or confectionery manufacturers, the "chick fever" has now subsided somewhat. But Maita is already pompously announcing even more perfect successors to the electronic cult objects, intended to keep her company in the front line of the competitive race against Nintendo, Sega and Sony.   V.F.

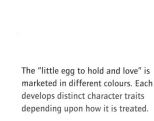

The "little egg to hold and love" is marketed in different colours. Each develops distinct character traits depending upon how it is treated.

PHILIPS-ALESSI LINE

Alessandro Mendini

Alessandro Mendini

In the autumn of 1991, two antithetical product design convictions met at a workshop in Groningen, the Netherlands. Present were engineers from Philips, with its director of the Department of Philips Corporate Design (the company think tank) Stefano Marzano and the creative designers grouped around Alessandro Mendini, long-time consultant for Alessi, the Italian manufacturer of kitchen accessories. While, for decades, the Italians have charged tangible, pragmatic, everyday objects with a poetic and narrative symbolism, the Dutch company stands for the development of helpful, functional, ergonomically optimized consumer electronics. The series of five kitchen appliances that arose from this cooperation of such dissimilar partners—a coffee-maker, hot-water cooker, juicer, toaster, and blender—unites sensuous Italian design with well-thought-out technical details. The appliances, soft in colour, sensuous in curves and pleasantly robust to the touch, house—depending upon their function—the most modern percolating technology: quiet motors, heating base, calcium filter or electronic sensors. Seen in the light of product language, these emotionally individualized, high-touch personalities belong not to the motto "form follows function," but rather to the principle—enhanced, if not completely and decisively replaced, since the Postmodern movement—"form follows fiction." Alberto Alessi, the eldest grandson of the company's founder and general director today, calls his company The Dream Factory, reflecting a specific strategy. Although The Dream Factory dominates with regard to the visual appearance of the appliances, the development of this kitchen line over the course of nearly five years would not have been possible without the technological experience and engineering prowess of the Philips development team. The results have not been without their many imitators: there is hardly a mixer, an electric toothbrush, even a vacuum cleaner, microwave or hair dryer that has not turned up with ice-cream colours and biomorphic forms. The logical and functional core of such appliances is thwarted and emotionalized by the casing: *animali domestici* (domestic animals). But, the Philips-Alessi line reacts to these imitations like diamonds to costume jewellery. Only through the ingenious combination of two different product philosophies could these sensational objects emerge. This is not in the least attributable to a comprehensive design-oriented research strategy that flowed into the project; from a marketing point of view, the corporate identities of both companies were enriched.   V.F.

These colourful, biomorphic kitchen appliances are jointly manufactured by Philips and Alessi: coffee-maker, hot-water cooker, juicer, toaster and blender.

VIRTUAL REALITY

Virtual reality is understood to mean computer-simulated reality, that is, a second, artificial world. Into this world, it would seem, one can immerse oneself with the help of the appropriate technical equipment. In contrast to everything that takes place on monitors in the guise of optically or acoustically retrievable information or interactivity (for example, during computer games), virtual reality delivers the full range of sensory perceptions experienced in the real world—sight, sound, smell, taste, motion, pain and temperature—as an analogous and simultaneously real experience, i.e. in "real time." Data transmission occurs via data helmets, data glasses and data gloves equipped with sensors for vision, sound and touch. In addition to these hardware devices, three-dimensional, fully detailed scenarios must be designed to create environments in which the virtual "infonaut" can navigate. Practical applications are on the rise, such as simulated driving scenarios in the automotive industry and applications for practising surgery procedures in medicine. Artists, athletes and astronauts are also exploring the potential of virtual reality. In terms of planning strategies, this technology is a useful tool for urban planners and architects, designers and set designers. With virtual reality the artificial reproducibility of reality—which began in photography and film on a two-dimensional level and reached a spatial dimension with holography, 3D-film technology (IMAX) and 360-degree surround-vision cinemas—is perfected to a psychological-physical experiential space.

In addition to economic uses, this technology harbours military and, above all, entertainment potential that is being developed currently by predominantly Japanese and American companies into virtual-reality equipment for the home. Aside from PCs and the Internet, virtual reality will be one of the most important data carriers of the twenty-first century.   V.F.

City planning, car testing, surgical techniques and space travel can be computer simulated.

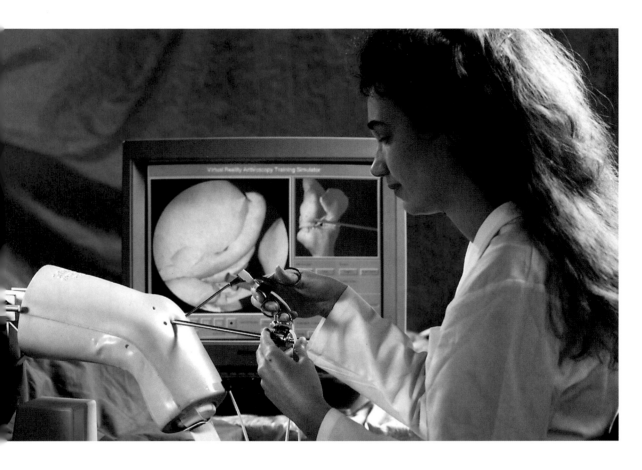

SELECTED BIBLIOGRAPHY

Underwood Typewriter No. 5, p. 14
Dingwerth, Leonhard. *Historische Schreibmaschinen*. Verl, 1993.

Hill House Chair, p. 16
Crawford, Alan. *Charles Rennie Mackintosh*. London, 1995; Garner, Philippe. *Twentieth-Century Furniture*. London, 1980.

Raleigh Safety Bicycle, p. 18
Caunter, Cyril Francis. *The History and Development of Cycles*. London, 1972; Bowden, Gregory Houston. *The Story of the Raleigh Cycle*. London, 1993.

Sitting Machine, p. 20
Hoffmann, Josef Franz Maria. *Josef Hoffmann: Architect and Designer*. Vienna/New York, 1981; Sekler, Edouard. *Josef Hoffmann*. Vienna, 1982; Noever, Peter. *Josef Hoffmann Designs*. Munich, 1992.

Ford Model T, p. 22
Hounshell, David A. *From the American System to Mass Production 1800–1932*. Baltimore/London, 1984; McCalley, Bruce. *Model T Ford: The Car that Changed the World*. Iola, Wisc., 1994; Simonds, Christopher. *The Model T Ford*. Englewood Cliffs, N. J., 1991.

AEG Electric Kettle, p. 24
Buddensieck, Tilman, ed. *Industriekultur: Peter Behrens und die AEG, 1907–1914*. Berlin, 1979.

Leica Camera, p. 26
Kisselbach, Theo. *The Leica Book*. Seebruck, 1967; Rogliatti, Gianni. *Leica: The First Sixty Years*. Hove, East Sussex/Cincinnati, Ohio, 1985.

Coca-Cola Bottle, p. 28
Candler, Charles Howard. *Asa Griggs Candler: Founder of Coca-Cola*. Alexander, N. C., 1997; Hoy, Anne H. *Coca-Cola: The First Hundred Years*. Atlanta, Ga., 1986; Watters, Pat. *Coca-Cola: An Illustrated History*. New York, 1978.

U.S. "Tunnel" Mailbox, p. 30
Bruns, James H. "Soap Boxes Won't Do." *En Route*. National Postal Museum Newsletter 5 (July-September 1996); Epstein, Rachel. *Mailbox U.S.A.: Stories of Mailbox Owners and Makers*. Salt Lake City, Utah, 1996.

Red-Blue Armchair, p. 32
Baroni, Daniele. *The Furniture of Gerrit Thomas Rietveld*. Woodbury, N.Y., 1978; Kouper, Marijke. *Gerrit Thomas Rietveld: The Complete Works*. New York, 1992.

Table Lamp, p. 34
Droste, Magdalene. *Die Bauhaus-Leuchte von Carl Jacob Jucker und Wilhelm Wagenfeld*. Frankfurt, 1997; Fiedler, Jeannine and Peter Feierabend. *Bauhaus*. Cologne, 2000.

Teaset, p. 36
Contemporary Designers. London, 1984; Neumann, Eckhardt, ed. *Bauhaus and the Bauhaus People: Personal Opinions and Recollections of Former Bauhaus Members and Their Contemporaries*. New York, 1970; Wingler, Hans M. *The Bauhaus: Weimar, Dessau, Berlin, Chicago*. Cambridge, Mass., 1969.

Wassily Chair, p. 38
Van Geest, Jan and Otakar Macel. *Stühle aus Stahl: Metallmöbel 1925–1940*. Cologne, 1980; Wilk, Christopher. *Marcel Breuer: Furniture and Interiors*. New York, 1981.

Rolex Oyster Watch, p. 40
Dowling, James M. *The Best of Time Rolex Wristwatches*. Atglen, Pa., 1996; Gordon, George. *Rolex*. Hong Kong/London, 1989; Rolex Watch Co. Ltd, ed. *Rolex Oyster*. Catalogue. Geneva, 1999.

Bugatti, p. 42
Kestler, Paul. *Bugatti: Evolution of a Style*. Lausanne, 1977; Saldern, Axel. *Bugatti: Kunstwerke auf Rädern*. Hamburg, 1991.

MR Chair, p. 44
Johnson, P. *Ludwig Mies van der Rohe*. New York, 1948; Calloway, Stephen. *Twentieth-Century Decoration*. New York, 1988; Museum of Modern Art, ed. *Ludwig Mies van der Rohe: Furniture and Furniture Drawings*. New York, 1977.

Side Table E-1027, p. 46
Adams, Peter. *Der Beistelltisch E 1027 von Eileen Gray*. Frankfurt, 1998; Constant, Carolin and Wilfried Wang. *Eileen Gray: Eine Architektur für alle Sinne*. Exh. cat. Frankfurt, 1996; Johnson, J. Stewart. *Eileen Gray, Designer*. Exh. cat. London, 1979.

Chaise Longue LC4, p. 48
Benton, Charlotte. "L'aventure du mobilier: Le Corbusier's Furniture Design of the 1920s." *Journal of the Decorative Arts Society* 6 (1982); *Le Corbusier Domestique: Furniture, Tapestries 1927–1967*. Exh. cat. Cambridge, Mass., 1992; Lotti, Luca. "Le Corbusier: Critica della stanza." *Domus* 691 (February 1988); Troy, Nancy J. *Modernism and the Decorative Arts in France: Art Nouveau to Le Corbusier*. New Haven, Conn./London, 1991.

London Underground Map, p. 50
Barker, Theo. *Moving Millions*. London, 1990.

Anglepoise Lamp, p. 52
Gardener, Carl and Barry Hannaford. *Lighting Design*. London, 1993; Myerson, Jeremy and Sylvia Katz. *Lamps and Lighting*. London, 1980; Sudjic, Deyan. *The Lighting Book*. London, 1985. www.anglepoise.uk

Bialetti Moka Express, p. 54
I segreti del caffè. Milan, 1995.

Volksempfänger (People's Radio), p. 56
Adam, Peter. *The Arts of the Third Reich*. London/New York, 1992; Selle, Gert. *Die Geschichte des Designs in Deutschland von 1870 bis heute*. Cologne, 1978.

Sparton Blue Moon Radio, p. 57
Teague, Walter Dorwin. *Design this Day: The Technique of Order in the Machine Age*. New York, 1940.

Zippo Lighter, p. 58
Amster, Robin. "Zippo Lighter." *Popular Mechanics* (August 1994); www.zippo.com/standard/about/history

Pencil Sharpener, p. 60
Bush, Donald J. *The Streamlined Decade*. New York, 1975; Loewy, Raymond. *Never Leave Well Enough Alone*. New York, 1951; Schönberger, Angela, ed. *Raymond Loewy: Pioneer of American Industrial Design*. Munich/New York, 1990.

Mercedes Silver Arrow, p. 62
Adler, Dennis. *Mercedes-Benz: 100 Years of Excellence*. Osceola, Wisc., 1995; Nitske, W. Robert. *Mercedes-Benz: A History*. Osceola, Wisc., 1978.

Kodak Baby Brownie Camera, p. 64
Collins, Douglas. *The Story of Kodak*. New York, 1990; Pulos, Arthur J. *American Design Ethic: A History of Industrial Design*. Cambridge, Mass./London, 1983; Teague, Walter Dorwin. *Design this Day: The Technique of Order in the Machine Age*. New York, 1940.

Hindenburg Zeppelin, p. 66
Dick, Harold G. *The Golden Age of the Great Passenger Airships, Graf Zeppelin & Hindenburg*. Washington, D.C., 1985; Nitske, W. Robert. *The Zeppelin Story*. South Brunswick, N.J., 1977.

DC-3 Dakota, p. 68
Francillon, René. J. *McDonnell Douglas Aircraft since 1920*. 2 vols. Annapolis, Md., 1988–90; Meikle, Jeffrey L. *Twentieth Century Limited: Industrial Design in America 1925–1939*. Philadelphia, Pa., 1979; Pearcy, Arthur. *Sixty Glorious Years: A Tribute to the Douglas DC-3 Dakota*. Osceola, Wisc., 1995; Pilgrim, Diana H. and Richard Guy Wilson. *The Machine Age in America 1918–1941*. New York, 1986.

Cord 810, p. 70
Beck, Lee. *Auburn & Cord*. Osceola, Wisc., 1996; Borgeson, Griffith. *Errett Lobban Cord: His Empire, His Motorcars*. Princeton, N.J., 1984; Butler, Don. *Auburn, Cord, Duesenberg*. Osceola, Wisc., 1992.

Fiat 500 Topolino, p. 72
Fiat 1899–1989: An Italian Industrial Revolution. Exh. cat. London/Milan, 1989; Giacosa, Dante. *Forty Years of Design with Fiat*. Milan, 1979.

Savoy Vase, p. 74
Alvar Aalto: Furniture and Glass. Exh. cat. MoMA. New York, 1984. Eidelberg, Martin, ed. *What Modern Was: Le Musée des Arts Décoratifs de Montréal*. New York, 1991; Schildt, Göran. *Alvar Aalto: The Decisive Years*. New York, 1986.

Minox Camera, p. 76
Heckmann, Hubert E. *Minox-Variationen in 8x11*. Hückelhofen, 1992; Moses, Morris. *Spycamera: The Minox Story*. Hove, Sussex, 1990.

Hardoy Chair, p. 78
Larrabee, Eric and M. Vignelli. *Knoll Design*. New York, 1981.

Volkswagen Beetle, p. 80
Iles, Rob. *The Beetle: The Chronicles of the People's Car*. Newbury Park, Calif., 1990; Reichert, Nikolaus. *VW Beetle: An Illustrated History*. Sparkford/Newbury Park, Calif., 1987; Shuler, Terry. *The Origin and Evolution of the VW Beetle*. Princeton, N.J., 1985.

Citroën 2CV, p. 81
Altena, Ernst von. *Citroën 2CV: The Ugly Duckling?* Sparkford/Newbury Park, Calif., 1988; Bieker, Josef. *Deux chevaux: Bilder aus der Enten-Welt*. Frankfurt, 1984.

Parker 51 Fountain Pen, p. 82
Dragoni, Giorgio and Giuseppe Fichera, ed. *Fountain Pens: History and Design*. Woodbridge, Conn./Milan, 1998; *The Fountain Pen: A Collector's Companion*. Philadelphia, Pa., 1997.

Lucky Strike Cigarette Pack, p. 84
Loewy, Raymond. *Never Leave Well Enough Alone*. New York, 1951; Schönberger, Angela, ed. *Raymond Loewy: Pioneer of American Industrial Design*. Munich/New York, 1990.

Wurlitzer Jukebox 1015, p. 86
Krivine, John. *Jukebox Saturday Night*. London, 1977; Lynch, Vincent and Bill Henkin. *Juke Boxes: The Golden Age*. London, 1981; Lynch, Vincent. *The American Jukebox: The Classic Years*, San Francisco, Calif., 1990; www.wurlitzer-jukebox.com/about/html

Vespa Motor Scooter, p. 88
Fanfani, Tommaso. *Una leggenda verso il futuro: i centodieci anni di storia della Piaggio*. Pisa, 1994; Leardi, Roberto. *Vespa: un miracolo italiano*. Rome, 1996; Sparke, Penny. *Italian Design: 1970 to the Present*. London, 1986.

Tupperware, p. 90
Clarke, Alison J. *Tupperware: The Promise of Plastic in 1950s America*. Washington, D.C./London, 1999; Zec, Peter, ed. *Frische in Form: Tupperware*. Essen, 1992.

Arabesque Table, p. 92
Bangert, Albrecht. *Italienisches Möbeldesign.* Munich, 1985; Brino, Giovanni. *Carlo Mollino.* New York, 1987; *L'étrange univers de l'architecte Carlo Mollino.* Exh. cat. Paris, 1989.

Univers Font, p. 94
Bardonnet, Blandine. *Adrian Frutiger: son œuvre typographique et ses écrits.* Exh. cat. Villeurbanne, 1994; Friedl, Friedrich. *Die Univers von Adrian Frutiger.* Frankfurt, 1998; Frutiger, Adrian. *Type, Sign, Symbol.* Zurich, 1980.

Lockheed Super Constellation, p. 96
Donald, David, ed. *The Encyclopedia of Civil Aircraft.* San Diego, Calif., 1999; Mellberg, William F. *Famous Airliners.* Plymouth, 1995.

Wooden Tray, p. 98
Berengo Gardin, Piero. *Tapio Wirkkala.* Milan, 1984; *House Beautiful*, January 1953, p. 27; Kras, Reyer et al. *Het Transparante Noorden.* Exh. cat. Amsterdam, 1999; *Tapio Wirkkala.* Exh. cat. Helsinki, 1983.

Ant Chair, p. 100
Arne Jacobsen 1902–1971. Exh. cat. Copenhagen, 1991; Toiner, Poul Erik and Kjeld Vindum. *Arne Jacobsen: Architect & Designer.* Copenhagen, 1994; Oda, Noritsugu. *Danish Chairs.* Tokyo, 1996.

Rolodex Rotary Card File, p. 102
Teague, Walter Dorwin. *Design this Day: The Technique of Order in the Machine Age.* New York, 1940, Patton, Phil. *Made in the USA: The Secret Histories of the Things that Made America.* New York, 1992.

Chevrolet Corvette, p. 104
Corvette: A Piece of the Action. Princeton, N.J., 1977; Mandel. Leon. *American Cars.* New York, 1982; Rasmussen, Henry. *Corvette: Eine Erfolgsstory in Bildern.* Königswinkel, 1997.

BIC "Crystal" Ballpoint Pen, p. 106
Alexiades, Alex. *The BIC Beginning.* Milford, Conn., 1990; Gostony, Henry and Stuart Schneider. *The Incredible Ball Point Pen.* Atglen, Pa., 1998.

Alu-Chair Series, p. 108
Kirkham, Pat. *Charles and Ray Eames: Designers of the Twentieth Century.* Cambridge, Mass., 1995; Neuhart, John, Marilyn Neuhart and Ray Eames. *Eames Design: The Work of the Office of Charles and Ray Eames.* New York/London, 1989.

Greyhound Scenicruiser, p. 110
Jodard, Paul. *Raymond Loewy.* London, 1992; Loewy, Raymond. *Industrial Design.* New York, 1979; Patton, Phil. *Open Road: A Celebration of the American Highway.* New York, 1986.

Ericofon, p. 112
McDermott, Catherine. *20th Century Design.* London, 1997; "Ericofon." *Design Magazine*, no.107 (November 1957), p. 27–28.

Braun Phonosuper SK4, p. 114
Burkhart, François and Inez Franksen. *Design: Dieter Rams &.* Berlin, 1980; Erlhoff, Michael. *Deutsches Design 1950–1990.* Munich, 1990; Wichmann, Hans. *System-Design: Bahnbrecher Hans Gugelot 1920–1965.* Basel/Boston, 1984.

Lego, p. 116
Uhle, Margret. *Die Lego-Story: Der Stein der Weisen.* Vienna/Frankfurt, 1998.

Barbie, p. 118
Boy, Billie. *Barbie: Her Life & Times and the New Theater of Fashion.* New York, 1992; Steele, Valerie. *Art, Design and Barbie: The Evolution of a Cultural Icon.* Exh. cat. New York, 1995; Tosa, Marco. *Barbie: Four Decades of Fashion, Fantasy, and Fun.* New York, 1998.

Morris Mini, p. 120
Nahum, Andrew. *Alec Issigonis.* London, 1988; Pomeroy, Laurence. *The Mini Story.* London, 1964.

Sony Portable TV 80 301, p. 122
Kunkel, Paul. *Digital Dreams: The Work of the Sony Design Centre.* Kempen, 1999.

Panton Side Chair, p. 124
Verner Panton. Exh. cat. Weil am Rhein, 2000.

IBM Selectric Typewriter, p. 126
"IBM's Selectric." *Industrial Design*, September 1961, p. 46–49; McQuade, W. "An Industrial Designer with a Conspicuous Conscience." *Fortune*, August 1998.

Braun Sixtant Razor, p. 128
Burkhart, François and Inez Franksen. *Design: Dieter Rams &.* Berlin, 1980; Erlhoff, Michael. *Deutsches Design 1950–1990.* Munich, 1990; Wichmann, Hans. *System-Design: Bahnbrecher Hans Gugelot 1920–1965.* Basel/Boston, 1984.

Arco Lamp, p. 130
Ferrari, P. *Achille Castiglioni.* Milan, 1984; Sparke, Penny. *Italian Design: 1970 to the Present.* London, 1986.

Samsonite Attaché Case, p. 132
Ballantine, C. J. *The Samsonite Story.* Oudenaarde, 1998; Shinn, Deborah. *Bon Voyage: Designs for Travel.* New York, 1986.

Brionvega Radio TS-502, p. 134
McDermott, Catherine. *20th Century Design.* London, 1997.

Harley Davidson "Easy Rider" Chopper, p. 136
Ball, K. Randall. *Easyriders: Ultimate Custom Bikes.* New York, 1997; Bolfert, Thomas C. *The Big Book of Harley-Davidson.* Milwaukee, Wisc., 1991; Hopper Dennis. "Bikes Were Always Work for Me." In: *The Art of the Motorcycle.* Exh. cat. New York, 1998; Leffingwell, Randy. "Harley Davidson Easy Rider Chopper." In: *The Art of the Motorcycle.* Exh. cat. New York, 1998.

Plia Folding Chair, p. 138
Bellati, Natty. New *Italian Design.* New York, 1990; *Italy: The New Domestic Landscape.* Exh. cat. New York, 1972; Sparke, Penny. *Italian Design: 1970 to the Present.* London, 1986.

Olivetti Valentine Typewriter, p. 140
Burney, Jan. *Ettore Sottsass.* London, 1991; Neumann, Claudia. *Designlexikon Italien.* Cologne, 1999; Radice, Barbara. *Ettore Sottsass: Leben und Werk.* Munich, 1993; Sparke, Penny. *Italian Design: 1970 to the Present.* London, 1986.

B&O Beogram 4000, p. 142
Polster, Bernd. *Designlexikon Skandinavien.* Cologne, 1999.

Tizio Table Lamp, p. 144
Bangert, Albrecht and Karl Michael Armer. *80s Style: Designs of the Decade.* New York, 1990; McDermott, Catherine. *20th Century Design.* London, 1997.

Sony Walkman, p. 146
Kunkel, Paul. *Digital Dreams: The Work of the Sony Design Centre.* Kempen, 1999; Morita, Akio, Edwin M. Rheingold and Mitsuko Shimomura. *Made in Japan: Akio Morita and Sony.* New York, 1986.

Philips Compact Disc, p. 148
Bekooy, Guus. *Philips Honderd.* Zaltbommel, 1991; Hesket, John. *Philips.* London, 1989.

In-line Skates, p. 150
Busch, Akiko. *Design for Sports.* New York, 1998; *Sport 90: An Exhibition about Design and Sport.* Exh. cat. London, 1990.

Carlton Sideboard, p. 152
Bangert, Albrecht. *Italienisches Möbeldesign.* Munich, 1985; Radice, Barbara. *Memphis.* Milan, 1984; Radice, Barbara. *Ettore Sottsass: Leben und Werk.* Munich, 1993; Sparke, Penny. *Italian Design: 1970 to the Present.* London, 1986.

The Face, p. 154
Brody, Neville. *G1: New Dimensions in Graphic Design.* New York, 1996; Wozencroft, Jon. *Brody: The Graphic Language of Neville Brody.* New York, 1988.

Costes Chair, p. 156
Albus, Volker and Volker Fischer. *13 nach Memphis.* Munich, 1995; Morgan, Conway Lloyd. *Philippe Starck.* New York, 1999; Starck, Philippe. *Philippe Starck: Mobilier 1970–1987.* Marseille, 1987.

Swatch Watch, p. 158
Swatch & Swatch. Exh. cat. Milan, 1991; *I Swatch Very Much.* Biel, 1983.

Apple Macintosh, p. 160
Bridek, Bernhard. *Der Apple Macintosh.* Frankfurt, 1997; Greenberg, Keith Elliot. *Creating the Apple Computer.* Woodbridge, Conn., 1994; Kawasaki, Guy. *The Macintosh Way.* Glenview, Ill., 1990; Linzmayer, Owen W. *Apple Confidential: The Real Story of Apple Computer.* San Francisco, Calif., 1999.

Motorola MicroTAC, p. 162
Motorola: A Journey through Time and Technology. Schaumburg, Ill., 1994.

Juicy Salif, p. 164
Albus, Volker and Volker Fischer. *13 nach Memphis.* Munich, 1995; Morgan, Conway Lloyd. *Philippe Starck.* New York, 1999; *Philippe Starck.* Cologne, 1991.

Internet, p. 166
Berners-Lee, Tim. *Weaving the Web.* San Francisco, Calif., 1999; Moschovitis, Christos J. P. et al, ed. *History of the Internet.* Santa Barbara, Calif., 1999; Porter, David, ed. *Internet Culture.* New York, 1997.

Bookworm Shelf, p. 168
Albus, Volker and Volker Fischer. *13 nach Memphis.* Munich, 1995; *Ron Arad Studio.* London, 1994; *Der Bookworm von Ron Arad.* Frankfurt, 1997.

Tamagotchi, p. 170
Betz, Doris. *Tamagotchi: The Official Care Guide and Record Book.* Kansas City, Kans., 1997; Crimmins, C. E. *Tamagotchi Egg.* New York, 1997.

Philips-Alessi Line, p. 172
Alessi: The Design Factory. London/New York, 1994.

Virtual Reality, p. 174
Ankstakalnis. Steve. *Silicon Mirage. The Art and Science of Virtual Reality.* Berkeley, Calif., 1992. *Art and Technology.* London, 1994; Levy, John and Rae Earnshaw, ed. *Virtual Worlds on the Internet.* Los Alamitos, Calif., 1998; Maher, Mary Lou et al, ed. *Understanding Virtual Design Studios.* Berlin/New York, 1999.

THE AUTHORS

V.A. Volker Albus is a professor at the Staatliche Hochschule für Gestaltung (State College for Design), Karlsruhe. An architect, exhibition organizer and journalist, he writes for various design journals and has published several books on design, advertising, popular culture and architecture.

D.B. Dorothy Bosomworth is a design and heritage consultant who lectures and writes on product history, design selection, development and trend analysis, and the conservation of historic buildings and their interiors. She is the author of *The Victorian Catalogue of Household Goods* (1991) and the *Encyclopedia of Patterns and Motifs* (1995) and a contributor to *Apollo, Architectural Review, Country Life* and *Crafts and Design.*

C.B. Christopher Breward is a professor of Historical and Cultural Studies at the London College of Fashion, The London Institute. He is the author of *The Culture of Fashion* (1995) and *The Hidden Consumer* (1999).

V.F. Volker Fischer is Curator of the Design Department at the Museum für Kunsthandwerk (Arts and Craft Museum), Frankfurt, an honorary professor at the Hochschule für Gestaltung (College for Design), Offenbach, and, from 1981–94, he was the assistant director at the Deutsches Architektur Museum, Frankfurt. He specializes in twentieth-century architecture and design.

F.F. Friedrich Friedl is a professor for typography at the Hochschule für Gestaltung (College for Design), Offenbach. Since 1969 he has published several books and organized exhibitions on the topic of contemporary typography.

C.H. Claudia Hellmann is a freelance journalist and a doctoral candidate in American Studies at the University of Munich, Germany.

R.K. Reyer Kras is the Chief Curator of Design at the Stedelijk Museum, Amsterdam, and the founder of the design firm, Aurelius industrial design.

C.L. Claude Lichtenstein, architect and curator, has organized many exhibitions and written numerous publications on architecture and design, including *Bauhaus 1919–1933* (1988) and *Stromlinienform-Streamline* (1992). He is currently a curator at the Museum für Gestaltung, Zurich, and a lecturer for design history and theory at the Hochschule für Gestaltung und Kunst (College for Design and Art), Zurich.

H.-U. v. M. Hans-Ulrich von Mende is an architect and a freelance journalist in the area of automobile design. He primarily writes for the *Frankfurter Allgemeine Zeitung* and has published several books.

J.C.M. Jane C. Milosch is an independent curator and art journalist living in Munich, Germany. She has worked as a curator for the Detroit Institute of Arts and the Davenport Museum of Art and is a foreign correspondent for *ARTNews.*

H.-H.P. Hans-Heinrich Pardey is an editor for the technology and automobile section of the *Frankfurter Allgemeine Zeitung.* He primarily contributes articles on bicycles, communications and computers.

R.S. Ray Sapirstein is a doctoral candidate in American Studies at the University of Texas at Austin. His major areas of concentration are in the history of photography and visual media, vernacular architecture and material culture.

J.S. Josephine Shea is Curator of Collections at the Edsel & Eleanor Ford House in Grosse Pointe Shores, Michigan, where she has directed numerous conservation and restoration projects. This historical house features the Ford family's fine and decorative arts collection as well as interiors designed by Walter Dorwin Teague.

C.S. Courtenay Smith is an independent curator and writer based in Munich, Germany. She was formerly Associate Curator at the David and Alfred Smart Museum of Art, The University of Chicago.

P.S. Penny Sparke is Head of the Design Conference at the Royal College of Art in London, organized by the Victoria & Albert Museum and the Royal College of Art. She has written numerous books on twentieth-century design and produced shows for radio and television.

J.St. Josef Strasser is a curator at the design museum, Neue Sammlung, Munich. He has taught design history at the Fachhochschulen (Technical Colleges) in Rosenheim and Munich and has published extensively on design and art history.

T.D.S. Thomas D. Sullivan was formerly the architectural critic of the *Washington Times.* Based in New York City, he currently works as a freelance journalist specializing in architecture and design.

J.M.W. Jonathan M. Woodham is Professor of Design History at the University of Brighton and Director of the Design History Research Centre, Brighton. He has written several books on contemporary design, including *Twentieth-Century Design* (1997), and is a founding member of the *Journal of Design History.*

J.Z. John Zukowsky is Curator of the Department of Architecture at the Art Institute of Chicago. He has published numerous books on twentieth-century architecture, including *Chicago Architecture: 1872–1922* (1987), *Chicago Architecture and Design 1923–1993* (1993), *Building for Air Travel* (1996) and *Japan 2000* (1997).

INDEX

Every effort has been made by the Publisher to acknowledge all sources and copyright holders. In the event of any copyright holder being inadvertently omitted, please contact the Publisher directly. We would like to extend our special thanks to the designers and companies who provided us with photo material.

p. 14: Deutsches Museum, Munich; p. 15: Leonhard Dingwerth, Bielefeld
p. 16 portrait: Glasgow School of Art Collection, left: The Glasgow Picture Library, right: Royal Commission on the Ancient and Historical Monuments of Scotland; p. 17: Mario Carrieri for Cassina, Milan
pp. 18, 19: Nottinghamshire Archives
p. 20 center: Vitra Design Museum, Weil am Rhein, top: Wittmann
pp. 22, 23: Ford AG, Cologne
pp. 24, 25: AEG, Nuremberg
pp. 26, 27: Leica Camera AG, Solms
pp. 28, 29: Coca-Cola, Essen
p. 30: Thomas Karsten, Vierkirchen/Munich
p. 31 center: Dieter Hellmann, Munich, bottom: Thomas Karsten, Vierkirchen/Munich
p. 32: Mario Carrieri for Cassina, Milan
p. 33 bottom left, portrait: Centraal Museum, Utrecht, bottom right: Frank den Oudsten
p. 34: Bauhaus-Archiv, Berlin, portrait left: Wilhelm Wagenfeld Stiftung, Bremen
p. 35 left: Bauhaus-Archiv, Berlin, bottom right: Erich Consemüller, Bauhaus-Archiv, Berlin, top right: Tecnolumen, Bremen
p. 36: Bauhaus-Archiv, Berlin; p. 37 top: Fred Kraus, Bauhaus-Archiv, Berlin, bottom: Alessi, Hamburg
pp. 38, 39: Bauhaus-Archiv, Berlin
pp. 40, 41: Rolex, Cologne

pp. 42, 43: Musée National de l'Automobile, Mulhouse,
p. 42 top right: Deutsches Museum, Munich,
p. 43 bottom left: VW AG, Wolfsburg
p. 44: Tecta, Lauenförde;
p. 45 top left: Tecta, Lauenförde, portrait: Bauhaus-Archiv, Berlin, bottom: Vitra Design Museum, Weil am Rhein
p. 46 top: Eileen Gray Archive, London, bottom: ClassiCon, Munich
p. 47: Vitra Design Museum, Weil am Rhein
pp. 48, 49: Fondation Le Corbusier, Paris
p. 49 top: Cassina, Milan
pp. 50, 51: London Transport Museum
p. 50 portrait: Holburne Museum, Bath, England
pp. 52, 53: Tecta, Lauenförde
pp. 54, 55: Bialetti Ind., Milan
p. 56 right: Sepha Wouda, left: AKG, Berlin
p. 57: Stedelijk Museum, Amsterdam
p. 58: Zippo, Bradford, Pa.
p. 59 top: pwe Kinoarchiv, Hamburg, center: Sepha Wouda
p. 61: Raymond Loewy Foundation, Hamburg
pp. 62, 63: DaimlerChrysler, Stuttgart
p. 64 bottom: Robert Opie Collection, London
p. 65: A. Bröhan for Die Neue Sammlung, Munich
pp. 66, 67: Archiv der Luftschiffbau Zeppelin GmbH, Friedrichshafen
p. 66 bottom: Ullstein, Berlin
pp. 68, 69: Deutsches Museum, Munich
pp. 70, 71: Auburn-Cord-Duesenberg-Museum, Auburn, Ind.
pp. 72, 73: Fiat AG, Frankfurt am Main
pp. 74, 75: Iittala, Iittala, Finland
pp. 76, 77: Minox, Wetzlar
p. 76 bottom left: pwe Kinoarchiv, Hamburg
pp. 78, 79: Stöhr, Besigheim

p. 80: Stiftung Automuseum Volkswagen, Wolfsburg, top right: Reinhard Köster, Berlin
p. 81: Citroën AG, Cologne
p. 82: Gilette, Baden-Baden
p. 83: Eckard Wentorf, Hamburg
pp. 84, 85: Raymond Loewy Foundation, Hamburg
pp. 86, 87: Deutsche Wurlitzer, Stemwede-Levern
p. 86 left: pwe Kinoarchiv, Hamburg
p. 88: Fondazione Piaggio, Pontedera, top right: Robin Davy, Munich; p. 89 top: Picture Press, Hamburg , bottom: Fondazione Piaggio, Pontedera
pp. 90, 91: Tupperware, Frankfurt am Main
p. 92: Bruno and Christina Bischofberger, Kuesnacht, portrait: Archivio Carlo Mollino, Turin
p. 93: Vitra Design Museum, Weil am Rhein
pp. 94, 95: Linotype, Eschborn
p. 96: Lufthansa AG, Cologne
p. 97: Lockheed Martin
p. 98 Portrait: Iittala, Iittala, Finland
p. 99: Stedelijk Museum, Amsterdam
pp. 100, 101: Fritz Hansen, Allerød, Denmark
p. 102 top: Newell Office Products, Wisc.
p. 103: Atlanta, Nettetal-Kaldenkirchen
pp. 104, 105: GM Europe, Rüsselsheim
p. 106, 107: BIC Germany
p. 108 bottom: Hans Hansen/Vitra, portrait: Eames Office, top right: Miro Zagnoli/Vitra
p. 109: Hans Hansen/Vitra
pp. 110, 111: Raymond Loewy Foundation, Hamburg
pp. 112, 113: Ericsson, Sweden
pp. 114, 115: Braun, Kronberg
pp. 116, 117: Lego, Billund, Denmark
pp. 118, 119: Mattel, Dreieich
pp. 120, 121: Rover, Neuss
p. 123: Sony Europe, Berlin
pp. 124, 125: Vitra, Weil am Rhein
pp. 126, 127: IBM, Stuttgart

pp. 128, 129: Braun, Kronberg
pp. 130, 131: Flos, Brescia, Italy
pp. 132, 133: Samsonite, Cologne
p. 134 top left: Alberto Venzago, top right: Serge Libis, bottom: Aldo Ballo for Brionvega, Milan
p. 135: Die Neue Sammlung, Munich
p. 136: pwe Kinoarchiv, Hamburg
p. 137: Randy Leffingwell
p. 138, 139: Giancarlo Piretti, Bologna
p. 140: from Design Process Olivetti 1908–1983, Frankfurt am Main, 1983, portrait: Sottsass Associati, Milan
p. 141 top: Sottsass Associati, Milan, bottom: Vitra Design Museum, Weil am Rhein
pp. 142, 143: Bang & Olufsen, Struer, Denmark
p. 144: Artemide, Milan, portrait: Serge Libis
pp. 146, 147: Sony Design Centre, Cologne
pp. 148, 149: Philips, Hamburg
pp. 150, 151: Benetton, Munich
pp. 152, 153: Memphis, Milan
pp. 154, 155: Philippe Starck, Issy-Les-Moulineaux
pp. 156, 157: The Face, London
pp. 158, 159: Swatch AG, Biel
p. 160: Apple, Munich, portrait: Frogdesign, Altensteig
p. 161 center: Frogdesign
pp. 162, 163: Motorola, Schaumburg, Ill.
pp. 164, 165: Alessi, Hamburg
pp. 166, 167: Internet
pp. 168, 169: Kartell, Milan
p. 170: Bandai, Cypress, Calif.
p. 171: Thomas Karsten, Vierkirchen/Munich
pp. 172, 173: Alessi, Hamburg
pp. 174, 175: Fraunhofer Institut, Darmstadt

Impressum

© Prestel Verlag, Munich · London · New York 2000

© of works illustrated by manufacturers, designers, artists, their heirs or assigns with the exception of: Peter Behrens, Ludwig Mies van der Rohe, Gerrit Rietveld and Wilhelm Wagenfeld by VG Bild-Kunst, Bonn 2000; Le Corbusier by FLC/VG Bild-Kunst, Bonn 2000.

Front Cover: Alvar Aalto, Savoy Vase, 1937 (Photo: Vitra Design Museum, Weil am Rhein); Gerrit Rietveld, Red-Blue Armchair, 1917–23 (Photo: Mario Carrieri, Cassina S.P.A.); Lego Building Block, 1958 (Photo: Lego, Billund, Denmark); Verner Panton, Panton Chair, 1960 (Photo: Vitra Design Museum, Weil am Rhein); Ettore Sottsass, Olivetti Valentine Typewriter, 1969 (Photo: Vitra Design Museum, Weil am Rhein); iMac, 1998 (Photo: Apple Macintosh). Back Cover: Raymond Loewy, Pencil Sharpener, 1933 (Photo: Raymond Loewy Foundation, Hamburg); Wilhelm Wagenfeld and Carl Jacob

Jucker, Table Lamp, 1923–24 (Photo: Vitra Design Museum, Weil am Rhein); Eileen Gray, Side Table E-1027, 1927 (Photo: Vitra Design Museum, Weil am Rhein); Le Corbusier, Chaise Longue LC4, 1928 (Photo: Oliviero Venturi, Cassina S.P.A.); Mercedes 300 SLR, 1955 (Photo: Daimler Chrysler archive); Dieter Rams and Hans Gugelot, Braun Phonosuper SK4, 1956 (Photo: Braun AG).

Frontispiece: Arne Jacobsen, Ant Chair, 1952 (Photo: Fritz Hansen, Allerød, Denmark). Other Illustrations: p. 8: Alvar Aalto, Savoy Vases, 1937 (Photo: Iittala, Finland); pp. 12–13: Tapio Wirkkala, Wooden Tray, 1951 (Photo: Stedelijk Museum Amsterdam); pp. 176–177: Ron Arad, Bookworm Shelf, 1994 (Photo: Kartell, Milan); p. 184: Philippe Starck, Juicy Salif, 1990 (Photo: Alessi, Milan).

Library of Congress Catalog Card Number: 99-069112

Die Deutsche Bibliothek – CIP-Einheitsaufnahme
Icons of Design, the 20th century / Hrsg.: V. Albus .... – München : Prestel, 2000
Dt. Ausg. u.d.T.: Design! Das 20. Jahrhundert
ISBN 3-7913-2306-7

Project Management: Sabine Thiel-Siling and Jane C. Milosch
Managing Editor: Jane C. Milosch
Production Editing: Claudia Hellmann, Jenny Marsh, Courtenay Smith and Danko Szabó

Translations from the German: Elizabeth Schwaiger and Robert Thomas
Translations from the Dutch: Arthur Payman

Photo Research: Stella Sämann

Prestel Verlag
Mandlstrasse 26, D-80802 Munich, Germany,
Tel. +49 (89) 381709-0; Fax +49 (89) 381709-35;
175 5th Ave., Suite 402, New York, NY 10010, USA,
Tel. (212) 995-2720; Fax (212) 995-2733;
4 Bloomsbury Place, London WC1A 2QA, UK,
Tel. +44 (171) 323-5004; Fax +44 (171) 636-8004

Design and Typesetting: Dorén + Köster, Berlin
Lithography: LVD, Berlin
Printing: Aumüller, Regensburg
Binding: Conzella, Pfarrkirchen

Printed in Germany on acid-free paper

ISBN 3-7913-2305-9 (German edition)
ISBN 3-7913-2306-7 (English edition)